# CHESTERTON CONTINUED
*A Bibliographical Supplement*

By the same author

*G. K. Chesterton. A Bibliography*

# CHESTERTON CONTINUED
## A Bibliographical Supplement

*by*

## JOHN SULLIVAN

*Together with some uncollected
prose and verse by*
**G. K. CHESTERTON**

UNIVERSITY OF LONDON PRESS LTD

SBN 340 09457 5

University of London Press Ltd
St Paul's House, Warwick Lane, London EC 4

Printed in Great Britain by
Hazell Watson and Viney Ltd, Aylesbury, Bucks

To
The Secret People

# ACKNOWLEDGMENTS

No one person has done more for the memory and reputation of G. K. Chesterton than Miss Dorothy Collins. No one interested in Chesterton calls upon her for help or advice in vain. Her discreet contribution to many of the books mentioned in these pages is considerable. My own debt to her is apparent. All but two of the items by Chesterton and all of the illustrations are from MSS in Miss Collins's collection. For her kind permission to include them, no less than for the ready access to that splendidly catalogued collection that I have enjoyed, I am deeply grateful.

For permission to include *Three Letters to E. V. Lucas* I am obliged to Dr Eamonn Norton and for *To the Jesuits* to the Master of Campion Hall.

To many friends and correspondents who have aided me in a variety of ways, my thanks are due, and in particular to: Mr A. D. Atkinson, Mr Patrick Cahill, Mr Norman Colbeck, Mr Evan Gill, Dr George E. Grauel of John Carroll University, Cleveland, Ohio, Dr Leo Hetzler, the Rev. P. Humbert Leers, O.F.M., Mr Aidan Mackey, Mr Anthony Rota, the Rev. Kevin Scannell, Mr Robin Skelton, Mr G. van Steenhoven, Miss Mary Sullivan, Mr Robert Walmsley, Mr Michael White, Dr Garry Wills, and Mr Antony Wood.

J.S.

# CONTENTS

# ILLUSTRATIONS

# INTRODUCTION

My attempt at a comprehensive record of the work of G. K. Chesterton in *G. K. Chesterton. A Bibliography* (University of London Press, 1958), was kindly received by critics both at home and abroad. There were some, however, who could not forbear to remark that, since Chesterton was no more than a journalist, he hardly merited the full bibliographical treatment. One reviewer wrote: 'the whole point of Chesterton . . . is that he achieved greatness not as an artist self-consciously creating an *œuvre*, but as a superb literary and metaphysical journalist'. The operative word is the last and, if not used here in a pejorative sense, it yet conveys to the reader something less than would 'writer' or 'author'.

This assessment was not a new one. Mr Michael White, in the *Dublin Review*, reminded his readers that James Stephens had said in a broadcast some years earlier that Chesterton was only a journalist who would be forgotten with the years—a judgment which Mr White rejected. Mr Sean O'Casey, in his autobiography, dismissed Chesterton in even stronger terms and, more recently, a new encyclopaedia of literature summed up Chesterton as a master who left no masterpiece. Contemporary histories of literature tend more and more to pass over Chesterton lightly and, as the years go by, the official recorders seem to be settling into general agreement that he may have been a good man who left no enemies but he was neither a great man nor a great author.

Fortunately, literary reputations do not always rest upon the findings of literary historians. Some writers endure because people obstinately continue to read them despite the best critical advice. Their immortality is of the kind indicated by Samuel Butler; they live, 'where dead men meet, on lips of living men'.

G. K. Chesterton died in 1936 and, with the notable exception of Bernard Shaw, no one of his great contemporaries is today so often quoted (with and without acknowledgment), referred to, remembered, or, I dare to say, so regularly read. *The Oxford Dictionary of Quotations* has seventy-nine entries under Chesterton, Bartlett's *Familiar Quotations* thirty-eight, and *A Treasury of Humorous Quotations*, fifty-two. The reviewer in *The Times Literary Supplement* of *The Faber Book of*

*Aphorisms* (Edited by W. H. Auden and Louis Kronenberger, 1964) wrote: 'Bacon, Blake, Chesterton, Goethe, Johnson, La Rochefoucauld Shaw, as expected, score highly'. In fact, Chesterton's score of sixty-two is surpassed only by Goethe, Dr Johnson and Nietzsche.

Of the dozen or so of Chesterton's books that are in steady demand, it is notable that *Orthodoxy*, *The Victorian Age in Literature*, *St Francis of Assisi*, the *Collected Poems* and the Father Brown detective stories did not have their origin in his journalism. The selections from his work in *Everyman* and similar series are regularly reprinted. Hardly a week goes by without its Chesterton reference or quotation in article or book and in a most remarkable variety of contexts. 'For the critics who think Chesterton frivolous or "paradoxical" I have to work hard to feel even pity: sympathy is out of the question. . . . In reading Chesterton I did not know what I was letting myself in for.' Thus C. S. Lewis, in *Surprised by Joy*. And of Professor Lewis, *The Times* obituarist wrote: 'But it will be universally admitted that he continues the tradition of Gilbert Keith Chesterton whose *Orthodoxy* had influenced him deeply'.

Since Lewis wrote, the tendency to mark Chesterton down as one who had shot his bolt between the wars and is of but slight, if any, importance to the modern reader can be discerned in the writings of the literary recorders. It is a typically Chestertonian paradox that this author, whose work is held by some influential literary critics to have been so transient, should so often and so readily come to the pen of modern writers. In the General Election of 1964, Mr Harold Wilson quoted Chesterton (*The Secret People*), was quickly charged in a Sunday newspaper with misquotation and the charge was as quickly refuted by an observant reader. In the same week, Chesterton provided the headline for the leading article in a political weekly. The columnist in another went to Chesterton for his *nom de guerre*. And if it be argued that Chesterton is thus quoted only by the older generation who were infected by him in their youth and, like C. S. Lewis, have never got over it, it is a distinguished younger critic, Mr P. N. Furbank, who, in discussing the novels of Miss Iris Murdoch, draws a parallel with Chesterton and employs the term Chestertonian, confident that the reference will have significance for his readers.

Another critic, Mr John Raymond, wrote in the *New Statesman*: 'Certainly, Chesterton's verse will be read as long as Kipling's—and that is saying a good deal. Men will continue to shout *Lepanto* as Buchan told the poet they shouted it in the trenches in '15. *Chuck it,*

*Smith!* and that wonderful Bronx cheer for Stratford-on-Avon ("Lord Lilac thought it rather rotten, that Shakespeare should be quite forgotten") have already passed into the tag lines of English literature. Alfred will be making his last stand at Ethandune long after the sun has gone down on Notting Hill and the Flying Inn. Adolescents will continue to take fire at *Orthodoxy* and their elders be stirred to contemplation by *The Everlasting Man*. . . . Personally, I think that his literary criticism—*Robert Browning, Robert Louis Stevenson* and *The Victorian Age in Literature*—is certain to survive. At his best he was a superb *jongleur* of ideas and *St Thomas Aquinas* is his greatest single intellectual achievement.'

Mr Peter Mulgrew, the mountaineer, told the present writer that on his three Himalayan climbs and the 1957-8 expedition to the South Pole with Sir Edmund Hillary, he took only one book with him: it was *Wine, Water and Song. The Penguin Book of Modern Verse Translation* (1966) includes Chesterton's version of du Bellay's sonnet *Heureux qui comme Ulysse*. The editor, Mr George Steiner, writes of this: 'at its best, the peculiar synthesis of conflict and complicity between a poem and its translation into another poem creates the impression of a "third language", of a medium of communicative energy which somehow reconciles both languages in a tongue deeper, more comprehensive than either. In the no-man's-land between du Bellay's *Heureux qui comme Ulysse* and Chesterton's English sonnet, so nearly exhaustive of the original, we seem to hear *"encore l'immortelle parole"*, Mallarmé's expression for the notion of a universal, immediate tongue from which English and French had broken off.'

And in 1963, that professional iconoclast, Mr Malcolm Muggeridge could write: 'It is surprising, in a way, that, when Chesterton was so often proved right in his judgments, he should still be less seriously regarded than contemporaries like Wells and the Webbs who were almost invariably wrong.'

Illustrations such as these of the range of Chesterton's talents, of his appeal to all sorts and conditions of men and of the enduring mark he has made on our literary consciousness could be multiplied in both number and diversity. Certainly, he is no longer 'fashionable'; but fashions pass.

Chesterton was, indeed, a journalist and never claimed to be anything else. But the plain fact is that, in so far as 'journalist' implies the ephemeral, the evidence (and he has now been dead for over thirty years) is all against those who employ the term to underrate his achieve-

ment. The publication of G. K. Chesterton. *A Bibliography* in 1958
evoked a response from readers of Chesterton in Great Britain, the
United States, Germany, Holland and elsewhere that confirmed me in
my belief that Chesterton, that great literary all-rounder, is still a force
to be reckoned with. In the ten years that have elapsed since 1958 there
have been published, in addition to an extended series of reprints of
his work, two new collections of his essays and a new pamphlet. The
critical discussion of his work in books and articles has continued un-
brokenly and there is now so much new material to hand that the time
has arrived when a supplement to the bibliography appears to be called
for. In bringing the record in the various sections up to date, with
additions since 1958, I have taken the occasion to incorporate some new
entries for earlier years and to add corrections and emendations
throughout.

It has also been possible, through the generosity of Miss Dorothy
Collins, the Master of Campion Hall and Dr Eamonn Norton, to
justify my title, *Chesterton Continued*, by including some interesting
examples of Chesterton's work in various styles which have not pre-
viously been collected and some of which now appear in print for the
first time. I hope that the reader, who will certainly turn to this section
first, will feel that in having these items thus made accessible, he has,
in this book, something more than a 'mere supplement' to the bibliography of a 'mere journalist'.

John Sullivan, Strawberry Hill, 1968

G. K. CHESTERTON

1874–1936

# CHRONOLOGY

## Chief events and publications

1874   29 May.   Born at 32 Sheffield Terrace, Campden Hill, W.8.
1887   Entered at St Paul's School.
1891–3   Contributes to *The Debater* (519).
1892   *The Song of Labour* published in *The Speaker* (558). First public appearance in print, while still a schoolboy.
1892–5   Attends Slade School and University College.
1895–1901   Employed by publishers (Redway and Fisher Unwin).
1900   *Greybeards at Play* (1).
       *The Wild Knight* (2).
       Meets Hilaire Belloc.
1901   Marriage to Frances Blogg.
       Becomes a regular contributor to the *Daily News* (till 1913).
       *The Defendant* (3).
1902   *Twelve Types* (4).
1903   *Robert Browning* (5).
1903–4   Controversy with Robert Blatchford in *The Clarion* (510).
1904   Meets the Rev. John O'Connor ('Father Brown').
       *G. F. Watts* (6).
       *The Napoleon of Notting Hill* (7).
1905   *Our Note-Book*. Weekly essay in *The Illustrated London News* (532) (till 1936).
       *The Club of Queer Trades* (8).
       *Heretics* (9).
1906   *Charles Dickens* (10).
1906–9   Controversy with Shaw and Wells in *The New Age* (542).
1908   *The Man Who Was Thursday* (11).
       *All Things Considered* (12).
       *Orthodoxy* (13).
1909   Removal from Battersea to Beaconsfield.
       *George Bernard Shaw* (15).
       *Tremendous Trifles* (16).

1910   *The Ball and the Cross* (17).
       *What's Wrong with the World* (18).
       *Alarms and Discursions* (20).
       *William Blake* (21).
1911   *Appreciations and Criticisms of the Works of Charles Dickens* (23).
       *The Innocence of Father Brown* (24).
       *The Ballad of the White Horse* (25).
1911–12   Contributes to *The Eye-Witness* (524).
1912   *Manalive* (27).
       *A Miscellany of Men* (28).
1912–23   Contributes to *The New Witness* (545).
1913   The Marconi Scandal.
       *The Victorian Age in Literature* (29).
       *Magic* (30).
1914   *The Flying Inn* (31).
       *The Wisdom of Father Brown* (32).
       *The Barbarism of Berlin* (33).
1914–15   Serious illness.
1915   *Letters to an Old Garibaldian* (36).
       *Poems* (37).
       *Wine, Water and Song* (38).
       *The Crimes of England* (40).
1916   October. Becomes editor of *The New Witness*.
1917   *A Short History of England* (43).
1918   Visit to Ireland.
1919   *Irish Impressions* (46).
       Visit to Palestine.
1920   *The Superstition of Divorce* (47).
       *The Uses of Diversity* (50).
       *The New Jerusalem* (51).
       Lecture tour in the United States.
1922   *Eugenics and Other Evils* (52).
       *What I Saw in America* (53).
       *The Ballad of St Barbara* (54).
       *The Man Who Knew Too Much* (55).
       Received into the Catholic Church.
1923   *Fancies versus Fads* (56).
       *St Francis of Assisi* (57).
1925   *G. K.'s Weekly* founded 21 March, and edited until 1936.
       *The Superstitions of the Sceptic* (59).

*Tales of the Long Bow* (60).
*The Everlasting Man* (61).
*William Cobbett* (62).
1926 *The Incredulity of Father Brown* (63).
*The Outline of Sanity* (64).
*The Queen of Seven Swords* (65).
1927 *The Catholic Church and Conversion* (66).
*The Return of Don Quixote* (68).
*Collected Poems* (69).
*The Secret of Father Brown* (71).
*The Judgement of Dr Johnson* (73).
*Robert Louis Stevenson* (74).
Visit to Poland.
1928 *Generally Speaking* (75).
*Do We Agree?* (352). Broadcast debate with Bernard Shaw.
1929 *The Poet and the Lunatics* (77).
*The Thing* (79).
Visit to Rome.
1930 *Four Faultless Felons* (83).
*The Resurrection of Rome* (85).
*Come to Think of It* (86).
1930–1 Second lecture tour in the United States.
1931 *All is Grist* (89).
1932 *Chaucer* (90).
*Sidelights* (91).
*Christendom in Dublin* (92).
1932–6 Broadcast regularly (536).
1933 *All I Survey* (93).
*St Thomas Aquinas* (94).
1934 *Avowals and Denials* (95).
1935 *The Scandal of Father Brown* (96).
*The Well and the Shallows* (97).
1935–6 Controversy (unfinished) with Dr G. G. Coulton in *The Listener* (536).
1936 *As I Was Saying* (100).
14 June. Died at Beaconsfield.

Published posthumously

1936 *Autobiography* (101).
1937 *The Paradoxes of Mr Pond* (104).

# BIBLIOGRAPHICAL SUPPLEMENT

This bibliographical supplement follows the style and order of *G. K. Chesterton. A Bibliography* and all references, unless there is a specific statement otherwise, are to that book.

While the parent work was going through the press in 1958, yet another collection of Chesterton's essays appeared, *Lunacy and Letters*. This was followed in 1961 by a pamphlet, *Where All Roads Lead* and in 1964 by another collection, *The Spice of Life*. Details of these, and of other post-1958 works relating to Chesterton, together with numerous items of earlier date of which I have learned since 1958, are given in the following pages. I have also taken the occasion to make a number of minor corrections and to include some supplementary notes. Additional items are marked with an asterisk.

Acknowledgment has been made on an earlier page of the generous help received from many friends and correspondents. I trust that all who have found the main bibliography useful will find this supplement equally so.

> I love to bask in sunny fields,
>   And when hope is vain,
> I go and bask in Baker Street
>   All in the pouring rain.

# A

## BOOKS AND PAMPHLETS BY G. K. CHESTERTON

### 1900

I. GREYBEARDS AT PLAY

*Amend* last line of entry to read:

'Published in October 1900 at 5*s*. BM 10 Oct. 1900.' and *add*:

'The advertisement on p. (103) gives the price as 3*s*. 6*d*. but all contemporary references are to 5*s*. Reprinted in the same month and the price reduced to 2*s*. 6*d*. In the reprint the advertisement for *The Wild Knight* is transferred from the last page to p. (103) replacing the advertisement for *Greybeards at Play* which now appears on p. (105) with "Ballads and Sketches" corrected to "Rhymes and Sketches" and the price to "Two Shillings and Sixpence, net."

Reissued, by Sheed and Ward, in October 1930, exactly thirty years later.'

*A note on Chesterton's first book*

*Greybeards at Play* was not included in *Collected Poems* and Chesterton makes no reference to it in the *Autobiography*. It was followed almost at once by Chesterton's first 'serious' book of verse (November 1900), *The Wild Knight*, and it is not difficult to understand how the latter has come to be regarded by some people as his first book.

This error is confirmed by the confident assertion of the publisher of *The Wild Knight*, Grant Richards, in *Author Hunting* (Hamish Hamilton, 1934):

'. . . I was the first publisher of G. K. Chesterton. But that was almost an accident. It happened in the following manner: R. Brimley Johnson . . . set up as a publisher . . . at much the same time as myself. But he hadn't much self-confidence and when it was open to him to publish a book of serious verse by a young friend, Gilbert Keith Chesterton, he brought the manuscript to me rather than run any kind of risk on his own

9

account. The book was *The Wild Knight*. Brimley Johnson liked it and why he did not whip up his courage was always an enigma to me, for he did publish the humorous *Greybeards at Play* later on. . . .'

Perhaps it was this circumstantial account that led E. C. Bentley into error in *Those Days* (Constable, 1940):

'His first book, *The Wild Knight*, was mainly a collection of these lyrics: its appearance, that unforgettable event in any writer's life, was in 1900. . . . In the same year was published his *Greybeards at Play*. . . .'

John Hayward, in *English Poetry* (Cambridge University Press, 1950) refers to *The Wild Knight* as 'Chesterton's first book of verse' and other writers fall into the same mistake.

For mistake it is: Grant Richards's account flies in the face of all the available evidence. *The English Catalogue of Books* gives October 1900 for *Greybeards* and November 1900 for *The Wild Knight*. The earliest reviews of *Greybeards* appeared in October, those of *The Wild Knight* in November.

It is certainly possible that it was *intended* to publish *The Wild Knight* first, for Edward Chesterton had paid Grant Richards for the publication in 1899—an event to which Richards makes no reference—and during the following five years Edward Chesterton wrote a series of letters to Grant Richards expressing his dissatisfaction with the way in which the book was being handled by the publisher. (See Maisie Ward, *Return to Chesterton*.) Whatever the intention, the first published book by G. K. Chesterton was *Greybeards at Play*.

*Opposite*

2. 'St Francis Xavier'. Milton Prize Poem, 1892, written at St Paul's School.

# St. Francis Xavier :
### the apostle of the Indies —

He left his dust, by all the myriad dead,
Of, you dense millions trampled to the strand,
Or 'neath some cross forgotten lays his head
Where of dark seas whiten on a lonely land:
He left his work; what all his life had planned,
A waning flame to flicker and to fall,
Mid the huge myths his toil could scarce withstand,
And the light died in temple and in hall,
And the old twilight sank and settled over all.

He left his name, a murmur in the East,
That dies to silence amid older creeds,
With which he strove in vain: the fiery priest
Of faiths less fitted to their ruder needs;
As some lone pilgrim, with his staff and beads,
Mid forest-brutes whom ignorance makes tame,
He dwelt, and sowed an Eastern Church's seeds,
He reigned a teacher and a priest of fame:
He died and dying left a murmur and a name.

He died: and she, the Church that bade him go,
Yon dim Enchantress with her mystic claim,
Has ringed his forehead with her aureole-glow,
And monkish myths, and all the whispered fame
Of miracle; has clung about his name:
So Rome has said: but we, what answer we
Who see in grim Indian gods and rites of shame
O'er all the East the teacher's failure see,
His eastern church a dream, his toil a vanity:

2.  THE WILD KNIGHT

In view of Grant Richards's account already quoted, it is interesting to note that the second edition of *The Wild Knight* came, not from him, but from Brimley Johnson and Ince, in 1905.

The poem on p. 48, *A Christmas Carol*, was issued later (n.d.) by Burns and Oates on a single folded leaf (page size $6\frac{3}{4} \times 4\frac{3}{8}$) with large rubricated initials.

### 1901

3.  THE DEFENDANT

Page 23. line 8. For '1903' *read* '1902'.
First American edition; New York, Dodd Mead, 1902, omits the note of acknowledgment and the title-page is a cancel.

### 1902

4.  TWELVE TYPES

In *Hatchards of Piccadilly, 1797–1947* Mr James Laver writes:

'G. K. Chesterton and E. V. Lucas, when they were both journalists on the staff of *The Globe* were much assisted by the firm which published their very early books: *Twelve Types* and *Catherine Anwyl*. The former was produced on hand-made paper in Hatchards' "Royal Library" and Chesterton was very anxious that he should be paid £25 for it at once, which, of course, was done. . . .'

Some copies were issued in different format for the Belles Lettres series of the Royal Library. They were slightly taller and carried on the front cover an overall gilt design of leaves surrounding six floral ornaments with lettering in smaller type, in two lines and without the author's name. The spine had two gilt rules instead of one, top and bottom. A. L. Humphreys, the publisher of *Twelve Types* was a partner in Hatchards.

**1904**

6.   G. F. WATTS

*Add*, p. 25:

C. Limp red leather. Back plain.

The Prospectus for *The Popular Library of Art*, issued in 1903, advertising the first five volumes, also announced *Wilkie* by G. K. Chesterton, as in preparation. This work never appeared. Nor was G. K. C. the author of two books credited to him in the same Prospectus: *The Defender* and *Critical Essays*.

First American edition: Chicago, Rand, McNally (n.d.).

7.   THE NAPOLEON OF NOTTING HILL

*Amend* lines 9 and 10 of entry to read:

*Copyright in | U.S.A.*, 1904.

At end of entry, *add*:

'A dramatised version by L. E. Berman, "based on an adaptation of F. D. Grierson and C. W. Miles" was prepared for perform-ance at the Royalty Theatre under the Vedrenne and Eadie management. It was not published nor, so far as I can discover, was it ever performed.

The typescript, prompt copies and other papers, including a letter undated from Chesterton's secretary, Miss K. Chesshire, approving the script, are in the Chesterton collection at John Carroll University, Cleveland, Ohio.'

**1905**

8.   THE CLUB OF QUEER TRADES

*Add*, after the eighteenth line of entry:

A. As described.

B. Back has a blind ruled border.

**1906**

10.   CHARLES DICKENS

At end of entry, *delete* full stop after 'Woollcott' and *add*:

'and the addition of Chesterton's article, *Charles Dickens: his life* reprinted from the *Encyclopaedia Britannica*. (359).'

## 1908

11. THE MAN WHO WAS THURSDAY

Binding variant:

D. Blue cloth lettered in black. Foot of spine reads: ARROW-SMITH / LONDON

All four bindings omit the full stop after 'K' on the spine.

First American edition, New York. Dodd, Mead, March 1908.

The edition in *Penguin Books*, 1937, includes on pp. 187–8:

'Extract from an article by G. K. Chesterton concerning *The Man Who Was Thursday* published in *The Illustrated London News*, 13 June 1936 (the day before his death).'

## 1910

17. THE BALL AND THE CROSS

p. 32. Below line 23, *add*:

'C. Stiff white pictorial wrappers printed in black and dark blue and lettered in white and black. All edges cut flush. Otherwise as B.'

Line 25. *Delete* 'Sheets o f the American edition . . .' to p. 33 line 3 '. . . save us'. *Add*:

'Four early books by Chesterton were published in America and England by John Lane:

|  | U.S.A. | G.B. |
|---|---|---|
| *The Napoleon of Notting Hill* | 1904 | 1904 |
| *Heretics* | 1905 | 1905 |
| *Orthodoxy* | 1908 | 1908 (but dated 1909) |
| *George Bernard Shaw* | 1909 | 1909 (but dated 1910) |

*The Ball and the Cross* was also issued in the U.S.A. by the John Lane Company, in 1909, but the English edition came from Wells Gardner, Darton in 1910 and is so dated on the verso of of the cancel title-page. The BM copy, however, was deposited three months before the actual English publication. It has no erratum slip and no cancels. The verso of the title-page reads: [*publisher's monogram*] | 1909 | *Copyright* 1906, *by* | *Joseph W.* *Darton* | *Entered at Stationers' Hall, London, England* | *Copyright* 1909, *by* | *John Lane Company.* | *Printed at the Trow Press, New York, U.S.A.*

The BM copy is in all other respects identical with the American edition. Page 93 has the misprint in line 6, "healthy working man", which is corrected to "healthy-looking man" by the erratum slip in A, B and C of the English edition.

Page 358, line 18 reads: "But God blast my soul and body" which, in the cancel leaf of A reads: "But Lord bless us and save us". This emendation is incorporated into the text in B and C. It is to be noted that A, B and C are all dated 1910, all have unsigned gatherings and no printer's imprint.

By courtesy of Mr Michael White I have now examined a copy of the "Fourth Impression, October 1925" which was "Printed in Great Britain". The gatherings are signed, there is no erratum slip and there are no cancels. But, whereas the correction on p. 93 has been incorporated into the text, the blasphemous utterance on p. 358, which had apparently been the sole reason for the cancel in A, appears unchanged, as in the American edition and the BM copy.'

18.   WHAT'S WRONG WITH THE WORLD

At the end of entry, *add*:

'A further comment by Chesterton on the title is to be found in the Preface to the American edition of *Alarms and Discursions* (20):

"The explanation is very simple; it is that in the modern world authors do not make up their own titles. In numberless cases

---

*Opposite*

3.   'The Troubadour of God'. Two of six verses, each with a drawing on the back, written about 1894.

# The Troubadour of God.

Out of three things
   I made a song
   A lark that sings.
In the thistles cozy,
A grey cloud loading
   The uplands grey.
    And a ~~bar~~ white bar boding
      —The break of day.

Out of three things,
   I made a song,
   The staff that swings
In my right-hand strong
A wind deep-throated
   The clouds that broke
   And a jest unnoted
      -A passer spoke.

*Opposite*

4. 'The Troubadour of God'. Two of six verses, each with a drawing on the back, written about 1894.

they leave the title to the publisher, as they leave the binding—that far more serious problem. . . . Some time ago, I tried
to write an unobtrusive sociological essay called "What is
Wrong". Somehow or other it turned into a tremendous
phillipic called "What's Wrong With the World". . . . Such
things arise from the dullness and langour of authors, as
compared with the hope and romantic ardour of publishers.
In this case the publisher provided the title and if he had
provided the book too I dare say it would have been much
more entertaining."'

20.  **ALARMS AND DISCURSIONS**

*Amend* last paragraph of entry to read:

'The American edition, published by Dodd, Mead, 1911, has a
two-page Preface and an additional essay, *The Fading Fireworks*.'

## 1911

22.  **A CHESTERTON CALENDAR**

Third paragraph: *for* 'Pp. (vi)' *read* 'Pp. (viii)'.

At end of entry (page 37) *add*:

'There is, however, confirmation of the advertisement in *A
Bachelor's London* by Frederic Whyte (*740A): "Among the
books which I devised [for Kegan Paul] was *A Chesterton
Calendar*, edited by Mrs Chesterton with just a little co-opera-
tion from me".'

23.  **APPRECIATIONS AND CRITICISMS OF THE
WORKS OF CHARLES DICKENS**

Paragraph nine (p. 38). *Delete* sentence in parentheses '(The
introduction . . . not included)' and at the end of this paragraph, *add*:

'The introduction to *The Uncommercial Traveller*, which was
published in the *Everyman* edition later in the year, is not included in the main text or listed in the Contents but it appears
at the end of the Introduction.'

25. THE BALLAD OF THE WHITE HORSE

*Amend* last lines of entry to read:

'. . . printed on hand-made paper and signed by author and artist, were issued at £2 2s.'

and *add*:

'Crown Book Edition. Pictorial wrappers. Illustrated and with an elaborate critical apparatus. Catholic Authors Press, Kirkwood, Missouri, U.S.A. 1950'

## 1912

27. MANALIVE

*Amend* last line on p. 40 to read:

'B. Green cloth, no lettering on front. Endpapers plain.'

28. A MISCELLANY OF MEN

Line 5 of entry: for 'four' *read* 'five'.

Last line of entry: after '*Preface*' *add* '(pp. v–x)' and after '*The Suffragist*' *add* '(pp. 1–9)'.

## 1913

29. THE VICTORIAN AGE IN LITERATURE

Paragraph eight of entry (p. 42) *add*:

'Top edges dark green'.

Paragraph nine: *for* 'fifty-nine' *read* 'sixty'.

*Add* new paragraphs:

'Revised edition, February 1914. Front and spine as A but stamped in black. T.e. plain. Printer's imprint on p. (iv) replaced by a list of six books "of kindred interest already published in the Library" and, at foot: *First printed, February* 1913 / *Revised and printed, February* 1914.

Issued, February 1914, at 1s. 3d. (cloth) and 2s. 6d. (leather).

The revision consists of minor corrections on pp. 32, 104, 115, 167, 168, 171, 174 and 220 occasioned by Chesterton's habit of

quoting from memory with slight variations. His remark on
p. 167, "I will quote only one verse (probably incorrectly)"
shows his awareness of this trait. The quotation, from *In
Memoriam, was* incorrect: it is corrected in the revised edition
but the warning in parentheses allowed to stand.

Later issues in the H.U.L. binding have the front blind-
stamped and the spine stamped in black.'

## 1914

### 32. THE WISDOM OF FATHER BROWN

First American edition: New York, John Lane Company, 1915.

### 34. LONDON

Third paragraph of entry, last line: *amend* to read: 'Top edges
trimmed, others uncut'.

### 35. PRUSSIAN VERSUS BELGIAN CULTURE

Last line of entry: after *'Everyman' add*: 'November 1914. (The
Triumph of the Degenerate)'.

### 37. POEMS

First American edition, New York, John Lane Company, 1916.
Title-page is a cancel.

## 1915

### 38x. THE SO-CALLED BELGIUM BARGAIN

*Amend* first paragraph to read:

SEARCHLIGHTS . . . No. 22 [*thin and thick rules*] / THE SO-
CALLED / BELGIUM BARGAIN / G. K. CHESTERTON.
/ [*rule*] / [*34 lines of text*] / [*thin and thick rules*] / NATIONAL WAR
AIMS COMMITTEE. / DISTRIBUTED BY W. H. SMITH AND
SON, LONDON: / BY JOHN MENZIES AND CO., LTD.,
EDINBURGH.

Third paragraph. After '*The Illustrated London News*' *add*: 27 July 1918.

Fourth paragraph. *For* '1915' *read* '1918'.

## 1918

*45x. WHAT ARE REPRISALS? / [*double rule*] / BY G. K. CHESTERTON [*all within an ornamental rectangle surrounded by a double rule*]

$8\frac{3}{8} \times 5\frac{1}{2}$. A single leaf, folded.

The title, as above, is set at head of text p. (1) which continues to foot of p. (4); below this, a rule and beneath: *Published by the Peace with Ireland Council, 30 Queen Anne's Chambers, London S.W. / Printed by the Caledonian Press Ltd. (T.U.), 74 Swinton St. London, W.C.1.—W* 847.

Date of issue and price (if any), unknown.

## 1920

49. OLD KING COLE

Second line of entry. After 'HE' *add*: ' ; '.

Fourth line. *Add* full stop after 'THREE'.

51. THE NEW JERUSALEM

First American edition: New York, George H. Doran, 1921.

## 1922

53. WHAT I SAW IN AMERICA

Page 56. At end of second line, *add* line division after 'SAW'.

54. THE BALLAD OF ST. BARBARA

At end of entry *add*:

'The American edition, issued by G. P. Putnam's Sons, New York, 1923, has a portrait frontispiece with protective tissue and a three-page "Introduction to the American Edition".'

55. THE MAN WHO KNEW TOO MUCH

> Lines 7–8 of entry. *Amend* to read:
>
> '(vi) *First published in* 1922 | *Printed in Great Britain.*'
>
> Page 57. Line 2. *Add* line division: G. K. | CHESTERTON

## 1923

57. ST. FRANCIS OF ASSISI

> Last line of entry. *Amend* to read:
>
> 'includes four of the coloured illustrations'.
>
> First American edition. New York. George H. Doran, 1924.

## 1924

58. THE END OF THE ROMAN ROAD

> First paragraph, third line. *Add* full stop after 'SERIES'.
>
> Fourth paragraph. *Add* 'A' before 'Light-blue cloth' and *insert* a new paragraph:
>
> 'B. Light brown soft leather with overlaps. Front stamped in gilt as A.'
>
> *Delete* last line of entry and *add*:
>
> 'Collected from *Out and Away* Vol. I, No. 1, July 1919.' (★549A)

★58A. 'THE UNIVERSAL | UNIVERSITY' | AN ADDRESS |

> DELIVERED TO THE ASSOCIATED SOCIETIES OF THE UNIVERSITY | OF EDINBURGH | ON 21ST NOVEMBER 1924 | BY | G. K. CHESTERTON | HON. PRESIDENT | [*ornament*] | PRINTED BY WILLIAM NIMMO & CO., 46 CONSTITUTION STREET, | LEITH, EDINBURGH
>
> $7\frac{1}{4} \times 4\frac{5}{8}$. One gathering of four leaves. Pp. 8. 1–8 text, with 'G. K. Chesterton' at end.
>
> Dark blue wrappers ($7\frac{1}{2} \times 4\frac{7}{8}$). Front lettered in black as above, insides and back plain. Stapled.
>
> Issued, November 1924.

## 1925

59. THE SUPERSTITITIONS OF THE SCEPTIC

First American edition: St Louis, B. Herder Book Co. (1925).

60. TALES OF THE LONG BOW

Lines 6–7 of entry: *amend* to read:

'(vi) *First published 1925 | Printed in Great Britain;*'

62. WILLIAM COBBETT

Fifth paragraph. Between 'Published' and 'November' *add*: '(undated)'.

First American edition, New York, Dodd Mead, 1926.

65. THE QUEEN OF SEVEN SWORDS

Binding variants. Five are listed. At end of B. entry, *delete* full stop and *add*:

'stamped in black: THE QUEEN OF SEVEN SWORDS reading upwards. No label.'

D. *Delete* comma after 'leather' and *add*: '. Front'.

*Delete* full stop after 'stamped in gilt' and *add*:

'THE QUEEN OF | SEVEN SWORDS | [*short rule*] | G. K. CHESTERTON within a small ruled frame, all within a blind border and a ruled border. Spine and back blank.'

## 1927

66. THE CATHOLIC CHURCH AND CONVERSION

At end of entry, *add*:

'Reissued in 1951 by Burns and Oates in stiff oatmeal wrappers lettered in red and black, at 5s.

A new edition, with two additional essays came from the same publishers in 1960 in their *Universe Books*, at 2s. 6d. Stiff, glossy wrappers, front lettered in red, black and white on a yellow background.

Publisher's Note, p. (5): "*The Catholic Church and Conversion* was first published in 1926 and reissued in 1951. For the present edition, two essays contributed to symposia in the same year are now reissued for the first time: *Upon This Rock* (from *An Outline of Christianity*, London, 1926) and *The Reason Why* (from *Twelve Modern Apostles and their Creeds*, New York, 1926)"

On its first appearance in *An Outline of Christianity* (★346B) the first of these essays was titled *Roman Catholicism*.'

67.  SOCIAL REFORM VERSUS BIRTH CONTROL

First paragraph, second line. Between '/' and 'G. K. CHESTERTON' *add*: 'BY'.

Fourth paragraph, third line. Between 'rule' and 'and' *add* a comma.

69.  THE COLLECTED POEMS OF G. K. CHESTERTON

Third paragraph, line four. *Delete*: '(1927)'.

Ninth paragraph, line 1. *For* '250 copies' *read* '350 copies'.

Line 3. *Delete* full stop after 'index' and *add*:

'but list of Contents is given in detail and "(1927)" added after "New Poems" on p. vii.'

70.  GLORIA IN PROFUNDIS

Paragraph six, second line. *Add* full stop after 'hand-made paper' and *delete* rest of this sentence.

At end of entry, *add*:

'First American edition, December 1927. 7 × 4¾. A half-sheet folded as four leaves and stapled to inner fold of grey wrappers. Pp. (8). (1)–(2) blank; (3) title page: GLORIA IN PROFUNDIS / BY / G. K. CHESTERTON / NEW YORK / WILLIAM EDWIN RUDGE / 1927. (4) *Copyright* 1927 *By William Edwin Rudge* /

---

*Opposite*

5.  'Lines to Waterloo Station'. Written about 1898, when G. K. Chesterton was working in Fisher Unwin's office.

# Lines to Waterloo Station.

### An Overflowing of feeling.

Come hither, Fisher Unwin
And leave your work awhile,
Uplooking in my face a span
  With bright adoring smile
All happy leaping Publishers
Round Paternoster Row.
Gay Simpkin, dreamy Marshall
  And simple Sampson Low
Come round, forgetting all your fears,
  Your hats and dinners too
While I remark with studied calm
  "Hurrah for Waterloo!"

Nag start not, fearful Putnam
  I sing no warrior's fall
(Macmillan, smile again, and dry
  The Tears of Kegan Paul)
But seldom on the spot I sing
  Is heard the peal of guns.

*Printed in USA*; (5)–(6) text; (7) *Twenty-seven copies printed | at the Printing House of William Edwin Rudge, | Mount Vernon, N.Y., December,* 1927. | *Twelve copies only for sale.* (8) blank.

Front wrappers lettered in black: GLORIA IN PROFUNDIS | BY | G. K. CHESTERTON.

An edition of the text only, issued to secure copyright.'

71. THE SECRET OF FATHER BROWN

At end of entry, *add*:

'The American edition, New York, Harper and Brothers, 1927, omits the dedication and is illustrated.'

73. THE JUDGEMENT OF DR. JOHNSON

First American edition, New York, Putnam, 1928. 'Judgment' is so spelled throughout and references to C. C. Martindale on title-page and at end of Foreword misprint 'S. V.' for 'S. J.'

74. ROBERT LOUIS STEVENSON

First American edition, New York, Dodd, Mead, 1928.

## 1929

79. THE THING

Fourth paragraph, second line: for 'left-hand' *read* 'right-hand'.
Last line of entry: for 'J.E.' *read* 'E.J.' [Edward Johnston]'.
At end of entry *add*:

'The quotation on the title-page is from Rudyard Kipling, *Puck of Pook's Hill* (*The Runes on Weland's Sword*).'

80. G. K. C. AS M.C.

Third paragraph, second line: *amend* to read: '*First published in* 1929 | *Printed in Great Britain*; v–viii dedicatory'.

## 1930

86. COME TO THINK OF IT

*Amend* last paragraph of entry (p. 77) to read:

'Most of the essays are collected from *The Illustrated London News*. The Introduction by G. K. C. celebrates his twenty-five

years of contributing "Our Note-Book" to that paper to whose
Editor, Captain Bruce Ingram, *Come to Think Of It* is dedi-
cated. The essays are selected and arranged by J. P. de Fonseka.'
First American edition, New York, Dodd, Mead, 1931.

### 87.  THE TURKEY AND THE TURK

At end of entry, *add*:

'"My first use of the zinc block was for *The Turkey and the
Turk*, by G. K. Chesterton. Carried away by Thomas Derrick's enthusiasm to illustrate this Chestertonian squib, we
went to enormous expense which we hoped, and still hope, to
recoup from a limited edition. This was the wrong way to
treat a firework which had already exploded in *G. K.'s Weekly*
and the popular edition with which we hoped to follow it is
never likely to appear."

H. C. Pepler, *The Hand Press*, Ditchling Press, 1934

The book of the original drawings, with the text written in by
hand and signed by author and artist was offered for sale at
100 guineas.'

### 1958

*112.  LUNACY / AND LETTERS / BY / G. K. CHESTERTON /
EDITED BY / DOROTHY COLLINS / SHEED AND WARD /
LONDON AND NEW YORK.

7 × 5. (A)–F in 32s.

Pp. 8, 192. (1) Half-title, (2) blank; (3) title-page, (4) *First
published* 1958; publisher's imprint, © *Dorothy Collins*, 1958
and printer's imprint; 5–6 *Foreword* signed D.C.; 7–8 *Contents*;
9–192 text.

---

*Opposite*

6.  First page of a fragment written about 1896. Published in *The
Coloured Lands*, Sheed and Ward, 1938.

I earnestly hope that all children will spoil this book by painting the illustrations: I wanted to do this myself but the publisher would not let me. But let the colours you lay on be violent, gorgeous, terrific colours, because my feelings are like that.

I have chosen the wonderful story of my friend the Admiral & his companions, to tell you, because of all the wise & good men I have known & loved the Admiral was, I do not hesitate to say, the easiest to paint with watercolours. You have only to colour his cocked hat & laced coat a strong prussian blue, & his trousers the same, leaving room for a great many gold buttons & gold stripes, but be careful or it will all go green & trickling. His face, which is rather like an eagle's or a lean parrot's, may be as burning red as you like, and his hair & eyebrows white, & under them a pair of eyes for which you must consult the little slip of directions they sell you with the paint box, to find out what colours are commonly used to express a look of ancient suffering transformed with immortal hope. You will find the ship under the paint brushes. The Admiral, you see, was a martyr of science, a pilgrim of truth, & one of those who live & die for one moment that may never come, the sight of a cape or the sudden colouring of a precipitate: if you do not understand this language, & I can only roughly render it by the phrase that there is no fool like an old fool. Shall I tell you the secret of the Admiral's life? He wished to discover America. His gay & thoughtless friends, who could not understand him, pointed out that America had already been discovered, I think they said by Christopher Columbus, some time ago, & that there were big cities of anglosaxon people there already, New York & Boston & so on. But the Admiral explained to them, kindly enough, that this was nothing to do with it. They might have discovered America, but he had not. He would take nothing superstitiously or on authority but wished to verify everything for himself. He had no proof even that "this island" as he used to call it, existed. But if it did,

Fine-grained, light-brown paper boards. Spine stamped in silver, reading upwards: S & W LUNACY & LETTERS CHESTERTON Front and back plain.

Published March 28, 1958, at 12s. 6d. 4,000 copies. BM 12 March 58.

'These essays appeared during the years 1901 to 1911 in the *Daily News*, mostly as a contribution to a weekly Saturday column. They have not appeared in book form before, although they belong to the period of similar collections, such as *Tremendous Trifles* and *Alarms and Discursions*, which account for about eighty essays chosen from more than six hundred.'

Foreword

## 1961

*113. WHERE ALL ROADS LEAD / BY / G. K. CHESTERTON/ (*C.T.S. device*) / LONDON / CATHOLIC TRUTH SOCIETY
6½ × 4⅛. One gathering of eight leaves. Stapled.
Pp. 16. (1) Title-page; (2) 40th Thousand / Extracted from a series *of five essays / contributed to* Blackfriars, 1922–23 / © *Dorothy E. Collins / Published by the Incorporated Catholic Truth Society, London / and printed by London Counties Press London and Uxbridge / Printed in England June, 1961 / AM*: (3)–16, text.

Paper wrappers. Front lettered in black and white on blue, sage green and orange: Do 326 / WHERE / ALL ROADS / LEAD / G. K. CHESTERTON [*so far, top left*] / 6D [*top right*] / [*Illustration of the dome of St Peter's (orange on sage green)*] / LONDON: CATHOLIC TRUTH SOCIETY Inside front wrapper, black on white, a statement about the Catholic Truth Society with rule at foot and, below the rule: *Cover design by Michael Tucker MSIA* Back wrapper, inside and out carries advertisements of C.T.S. publications.

Published in June, 1961 at 6d. 40,000 copies.

## 1964

*114. THE SPICE OF LIFE / AND OTHER ESSAYS / BY / G. K. CHESTERTON / EDITED BY / DOROTHY COLLINS / 1964 / DARWEN FINLAYSON / BEACONSFIELD
7⅝ × 5. [A] to L in eights.
Pp. 8, 176. (1) Half-title, (2) blank; (3) title-page, (4) *First*

*published* 1964 | *by Darwen Finlayson Limited* | *Beaconsfield,
Bucks.* | *Copyright* © *Dorothy E. Collins* | *Set in* 11 *on* 12 *pt
Baskerville* | *Printed in Great Britain by* | *Cox and Wyman, Ltd* |
*London, Fakenham and Reading*; (5) Editor's note, (6) blank;
7–(8) Contents; 9–171 text, 172–175 sources, (176) blank.

Frontispiece, tipped in: *To the Editor. Inscription in a copy of*
Christendom in Dublin *presented by G.K.C. to Dorothy Collins,*
1932.

Light-blue grained cloth. Front and back blank. Spine stamped
in gilt: THE | SPICE | OF | LIFE | G. K. | CHESTERTON |
DARWEN | FINLAYSON

Pictorial dust jacket lettered in red and black carries a study of
G. K. Chesterton by James Gunn.

Published 17 November 1964. 2,500 copies. BM 20 Nov. 1964.

'These essays cover a wide range of time and source. *The
Spice of Life* was written only three months before G. K.
Chesterton died. None of them has appeared in a collection
before.

D. E. C.'

Note on p. (5)

The essays are presented in five groups: Essays on Literature in
General; On Particular Books and Writers; Thought and
Belief; At Home and Abroad; The Spice of Life. They are
collected from: *Academy, Daily News, G. K.'s Weekly, The
Illustrated London News, John O'London's Weekly, Lending
Library and Book Borrower's Record, The Listener, New Witness,
New York American, Speaker,* and *T. P.'s Weekly*; and from the
following books: *Essays of the Year* 1931–2 (385), *Encyclopaedia
Britannica* (359), *King Lear* (368), *Aesop's Fables* (259), *Charlotte
Brontë* 1816–1916 (285), *An Outline of Christianity* (346B), *The
Venture* (208).

---

*Opposite*

7.   'A Song of Wild Fruit'. Written for Dorothy Collins in thanks
for the gift of a pineapple, 1929. Published in *The Coloured Lands*,
Sheed and Ward, 1938.

# A Song of Wild Fruit.

The Pineapple knows nothing
Of the Apple or the Pine.
The Grape-Fruit is a fruit: but not
The God's fruit of the Vine.
And Grape-nuts are not even Nuts
In the Hygienic Hut
Where the Nut, Crank with the Nut-crackers
Is cracking his own nut.

Far in the land of Nouveaux Names
These antic fruits were born,
Where men gather grapes of thistles
And the figs grow on the thorn.
And Ananias named the fruit
That Frenchmen call Ananas.
And all the Plantains are a plant,
And .....NO! WE have Bananas!

# B
## BOOKS AND PAMPHLETS CONTAINING
## CONTRIBUTIONS BY G. K. CHESTERTON

### 1902

201. THOMAS CARLYLE

Third paragraph, line six.

*Delete* comma after 'illustrations' *add* full stop and *delete* rest of the sentence.

202. ROBERT LOUIS STEVENSON

*Delete* the heading '1903' above this entry.

*Add* square brackets thus: [By W. Robertson Nicoll and G. K. Chesterton].

Fifth line. *For* 'November' *read* '1903'.

203. LEO TOLSTOY

*Add*, as heading above this entry:

### '1903'

*Delete* 'and Edward Garnett'.

*Add*, after, 'Perris': 'Etc. [*Edward Garnett*]'.

208. THE VENTURE

*Add*, at end of entry: '(114).'

### 1904

213. ENGLAND: A NATION

A leaflet, $8 \times 5\frac{1}{8}$ is sometimes to be found loosely inserted. Headed 'The Patriots' Club / President G. K. Chesterton', it outlines the aims and objects of the club in five paragraphs. A note at the foot states: 'The Patriots' Club will endeavour to carry out its objects by means of a volume of essays (to be announced shortly), occasional pamphlets, public meetings and other recognised means of agitation and advertisement. . . .

Hon. Secretary: Lucian Oldershaw, 1 Sheffield Terrace, Campden Hill, W.'

Two meetings were held in 1902, on 9 January and 25 March. Conrad Noel and C. F. G. Masterman were members. Apart from *England: A Nation* there were no other publications.

215. MR. CROWLEY AND THE CREEDS AND THE CREED OF MR. CHESTERTON

At end of entry, *add*:

'This eight-page "postscript" was issued as a loose insert in *Why Jesus Wept* (702A).'

## 1905

*217A. LETTERS ADDRESSED TO A. P. WATT

A. P. Watt and Son.

Contains a letter (p. 40), written from 60 Overstrand Mansions, Battersea, and undated, to A. P. Watt, Chesterton's agent. (See 364.)

## 1907

*221A. BRONTË SOCIETY PUBLICATIONS. PART XVI

Transactions: containing Report of Proceedings at Bradford and Ilkley, A Paper Read before the Society and other Matters.

Printed for the Society by M. Field & Sons, Ltd., Southgate, Bradford. March 1907.

Contains: *Charlotte Brontë and the Realists*. The substance of an address delivered by Mr. Gilbert K. Chesterton at the Annual General Meeting, at Ilkley, on 26 January 1907, pp. 6–11.

223. THE BOOK OF JOB

Between lines two and three *add*: 'Also 25 copies on Japanese vellum'.

## 1910

254. EYES OF YOUTH

Revise entry to read: 'A Book of Verse by Padraic Colum. Shane Leslie. Viola Meynell. Ruth Lindsay. Hugh Austin. Judith Lytton. Olivia Meynell. Maurice Healy. Monica

Saleeby. & Francis Meynell. With four early Poems by Francis Thompson, & a Foreword by Gilbert K. Chesterton. Herbert and Daniel *Foreword* pp. vii–x.'

## 1911

256. THE UNCOMMERCIAL TRAVELLER

Third line. *Add*: '(23)' at end.

*Delete* lines four and five.

*257A. RES PAULINAE. The Eighth Half-Century of St Paul's School. Edited by Rev. R. B. Gardiner, M.A. Formerly Surmaster and John Lupton, M.A. Lately Assistant Master. St Paul's School, West Kensington. Contains: *XXIII The School Magazines* By G. K. Chesterton (1887–1892) pp. 237–42.

*257B. WOMEN'S SUFFRAGE AND MILITANCY Edited by Huntley Carter. Frank Palmer (n.d.). Contains: replies by G. K. C. to four questions, p. 11.

## 1914

265. A CLUSTER OF GRAPES

Second line. *For* 'collected' *read* 'collated'.

267. CHRISTIANA AND HER CHILDREN

Third line. *For* 'Tailh' *read* 'Taith'.

268. DO MIRACLES HAPPEN?

At end of entry *add*:

'The discussion took place during the run of *Magic* at the Little Theatre.'

## 1916

277. COTTAGE ECONOMY

*Revise* entry to read:

'COTTAGE ECONOMY. By William Cobbett. With an Introduction by G. K. Chesterton. Published by Douglas

Pepler At The Hampshire House Workshops. May. 250 copies. *Introduction,* pp. (iii)–vi.

1926 Reissued by Peter Davies Ltd. The facsimile of the title-page of the 17th (1850) edition of Cobbett's book is omitted and the Introduction is restyled "Preface" on dust-jacket, title-page and at the head of the text.'

281. RAEMAKERS' CARTOONS

*Revise* entry to read:

'*Land and Water.* Issued in 26 fortnightly parts, 23 February 1916 to 8 February 1917, with commentaries on the cartoons by various hands. Those by G. K. Chesterton were: Part 1, 23 Feb. 1916: *Satan's Partner; Europe* 1916. Part 2, 9 March: *Miss Cavell.* Part 3, 23 March: *Seduction.* Part 4, 6 April: *The Great Surprise.* Part 6, 4 May: *Ferdinand the Chameleon.* Part 9, 15 June: *The Dutch Journalist to his Belgian Confrère.* Part 11, 13 July: *Easter* 1915. Part 14, 24 August: *The Beginning of the Expiation.* Part 15, 7 Sept.: *Gallipoli.* Part 16, 21 Sept.: *Peace Reigns at Dinant.* Part 19, 2 Nov.: *Five on a Bench.*

Issued in two volumes, Vol. I (Parts 1–13), in 1916 and Vol. II (Parts 14–26) early in 1917.'

283. THE BOOK OF ITALY

Between 'Picolli.' and 'New York', *add*: 'London, T. Fisher Unwin.'

*283A. THE UNSCATHED CRUCIFIX or The War and Human Suffering. By A. H. Baverstock, M.A., Rector of Hinton Martel. . . . With a Preface by Gilbert K. Chesterton. London: Faith Press. Milwaukee: Young Churchman Co. Preface, pp. 3–10.

### 1917

285. CHARLOTTE BRONTË, 1816–1916

After 'Brontë Society' *add*: 'Edited by Butler Wood, F.R.S.L.' For 'pp. 49–54' *read* 'pp. 47–54'.

At end of entry *add*: '(114)'.

## 1919

291. A HISTORY OF THE UNITED STATES
>    At end of entry, *add*:
>
>    '1940. New edition, edited by D. W. Brogan. Dent. *Everyman Library*. The Introduction by G. K. Chesterton is retitled: *Biographical Note on the Author*.'

293. THE SONG OF ROLAND
>    At end of entry, *add*:
>
>    '1959. Reissued in Ann Arbor Paperbacks. University of Michigan Press. *Introduction*, pp. vii–x.'

297. A MISCELLANY OF POETRY, 1919
>    At end of entry, *add*:
>
>    'The poems here printed are new in the sense that they have not previously been issued by their authors in book form. . . .'
>
>    Prefatory Note

## 1920

*299A. THE SOCIETY FOR THE PROTECTION OF ANCIENT BUILDINGS. Forty-Third Annual Report of the Committee; the General Meeting of the Society, and a Paper read by Mr G. K. Chesterton, July 1920. A. R. Powys, Secretary, 20 Buckingham Street, Adelphi, London, W.C.2. Contains: Mr Chesterton's Speech, pp. 45–57.

## 1922

*306A. LETTERS ON POLISH AFFAIRS. By Charles Sarolea. Edinburgh. Oliver and Boyd. Contains: Introduction by G. K. Chesterton, pp. 7–12.

## 1923

*307A. A MISCELLANY OF POETRY, 1920–22. Edited by William Kean Seymour. Cecil Palmer and Hayward. Contains: *The Sword of Surprise*. (Collected in 54.)
>    '. . . restricted to poems which have not so far, appeared in book form.'
>
>    Prefatory Note

310. THE OUTLINE OF LITERATURE

> *Amend* entry to read:
>
> 'THE OUTLINE OF LITERATURE. Edited by John Drinkwater. Newnes. Two volumes. (n.d.) Contains: Vol. II, Chapter XXX, pp. 464–80. *Dickens and Thackeray*. In the later, one-volume edition, pp. 677–99.'

## 1924

*317A. THE BRITISH LEGION ALBUM in aid of Field Marshal Earl Haig's Appeal for Ex-Service Men of All Ranks. Compiled by E. Lonsdale Deighton. Cassell. Contains: *A Quotation* in facsimile holograph.

319. THE UN-DIVINE COMEDY

> After 'Krasinski' *add*:
>
> 'Translated by Harriette E. Kennedy, B.A., and Zofia Uminska. Preface by G. K. Chesterton. Introduction by Artur Gorski. London.'

323. THE BOOK OF THE QUEEN'S DOLL'S HOUSE

> At end of entry *add*: 'Edition limited to 1,500 numbered copies.'

326. THE BOOK OF THE MICROCOSM

> After 'Privately printed' *add*: 'North Country Press.'
>
> At end of entry *add*:
>
> 'Also 50 numbered copies on hand-made paper.'

*326B. THEATRE ROYAL, DRURY LANE. Programme and News-Sheet of 'A Midsummer Night's Dream'. Contains: *A Midsummer Night's Dream* (pp. [7]–[8]).

## 1925

330. THE WRONG LETTER

> Issued, not in 1925, as given, but in 1926.

## 1926

335. CHOSEN POEMS

At end of third line of entry, *add*:

'Also a special edition on Japanese vellum, limited to 100 copies.'

*338A. BEACONSFIELD: OFFICIAL GUIDE BOOK. By Thos. F. Lane. With an Introduction by G. K. Chesterton. Beaconsfield Urban District Council. September.

341. TWELVE MODERN APOSTLES AND THEIR CREEDS

*Delete*: '(550)'.

*346B. AN OUTLINE OF CHRISTIANITY. Edited by A. S. Peake. Five volumes. Waverley Book Co. Contains: *Roman Catholicism* Vol. III, pp. 124–31 and *Anti-Religious Thought in the Eighteenth Century* Vol. IV, pp. 21–7.

*346C. WONDERFUL LONDON. Edited by St John Adcock. Three volumes. Fleetway House. (n.d.) Contains: Vol. 3, Chapter LXXVI, pp. 771–7, *The Case for Old London*.
1935. Silver Jubilee edition in one volume. Chapter XXXII, pp. 206–12.

## 1928

354. THE GOLDEN ARROW

The *Introduction* by G. K. Chesterton also appeared in the edition illustrated by Norman Hepple issued by Cape in November 1930, pp. 11–14.

355. DRINKING SONGS AND OTHER SONGS

*Add*: 'There was also a "Signed Edition" of 100 numbered copies.'

## 1929

359. THE ENCYCLOPAEDIA BRITANNICA

At end of entry *add*:

'*Charles Dickens* was reprinted in *Charles Dickens, the Last of the Great Men* (see 10) and *Humour* was collected in *The Spice of Life* (114).'

361. CATHOLIC EMANCIPATION, 1829–1929

   *Revise* entry to read:

'CATHOLIC EMANCIPATION, 1829 to 1929. Essays by Various Writers. With an Introduction by His Eminence Cardinal Bourne. Longmans, Green. Contains: *XIII, The Outlook.* pp. 267–(281).'

364. LETTERS ADDRESSED TO A. P. WATT AND HIS SONS 1883–1929

   *Add*: 'A later issue of 217A with additional letters and a slight change of title. A second letter from Chesterton is included, addressed to H. Watt and dated February 23 [1922].'

*364A. CHRISTMAS BOOKS. By Charles Dickens. Introduction by G. K. Chesterton. Collins. Library of Classics. (n.d.)

The Introduction to this volume is by D. N. Brereton M.A. It is preceded by a general introduction to Dickens: *Dickens, A Survey* by G. K. Chesterton (pp. v–xi).

**1930**

366. VANITY FAIR

   *Revise entry to read:*

'VANITY FAIR, A Novel Without a Hero. By William Makepeace Thackeray. Introduction by G. K. Chesterton. Illustrations by John Austen. Oxford. Printed for the Limited Editions Club by the Oxford University Press, 1931. Two volumes, boxed. Edition limited to 1,500 copies signed by the artist. Issued by the Limited Editions Club, New York. *Introduction*, Vol. I, pp. (v)–xii.

The Introduction was reprinted in *A Book of Prefaces*, The Limited Editions Club, New York, 1941, and collected in *A Handful of Authors*, 1953 (110).'

368. KING LEAR.

   At end of entry *add*: '(114)'.

## 1931

### 374. MARGARET DOUGLAS

*Delete* 'Hilaire Belloc' to end of entry and *add*:

'Charlotte Balfour, Hilaire Belloc, G. K. Chesterton, John McCullum, Nesta Sawyer, and by her husband for whom this book has been printed By H. D. C. Pepler Ditchling Common Sussex September 1931.

Edition limited to 150 numbered copies printed on handmade paper on a Stanhope hand-press, and the type distributed. (St Dominic's Press). Contains: a poem, *In Memoriam M.D.* p. (285).'

### 378A. THE MERCURY BOOK OF VERSE

*Sonnets in Summer Heat* were also reprinted in 1931 in *The Best Poems of* 1930. Selected by Thomas Moult and decorated by Elizabeth Montgomery. Cape. pp. 32–3.

## 1932

### 385. ESSAYS OF THE YEAR, 1931–1932

At end of entry, *add*: '(114)'.

### 387. THE PENN COUNTRY OF BUCKINGHAMSHIRE

*Delete*: 'Also . . . *de luxe*'.

*Add*: 'Also a specially printed edition of fifty copies. Published for the "Penn Country" branch of the Council for the Preservation of Rural England.'

*Add* the following entry immediately below the heading '**1933**' on page 117:

### *389B. THE JOHNSON SOCIETY OF LONDON.

REPORT OF THE SPEECHES on the occasion of the Third Annual Dinner at the Criterion Restaurant, London, on Tuesday, 26 January 1932. London: Published by the Johnson Society of London, 1933. Price One Shilling and Sixpence. Contains: *Mr G. K. Chesterton's speech*, pp. 6–11.

399. PAULINE AND OLD PAULINE, 1884–1931
   For 'Henry' read 'Hubert'.

   Add the following entry immediately below '1934' on page
   118:
*399A. SOME APPRECIATIONS OF WILLIAM MORRIS.
   24 March 1934. Edited by Geo. Ed. Roebuck. Issued by request
   of the Borough Council. Published by the Walthamstow
   Antiquarian Society. January 1934. Contains: a brief tribute to
   William Morris by G. K. Chesterton, p. 13.

### 1936
408. A. R. ORAGE: A MEMOIR
   At end of entry, add:
   'The Introduction had appeared as an obituary article on Orage
   in the New English Weekly, 15 November 1934.'

*408A. GERMANY'S NATIONAL RELIGION with a Fore-
   word by G. K. Chesterton. 'Friends of Europe' Publications
   No. 13. Issued by Friends of Europe, 122 St Stephens House,
   London, S.W. [n.d.] Foreword, pp. (3)–(5).

### 1938
*409X. LEADERS AND PAGES. Edited by A. R. Moon M.A.
   and G. H. McKay B.A. Longmans, Green. Contains: Crime
   Among the Teacups (pp. 14–18) reprinted from The Illustrated
   London News (23 May 1936) and Extremes Meet (pp. 177–81)
   from The Illustrated London News (20 July 1935) collected in
   As I Was Saying (100) under the title About the Workers.

*409Y. THE OPEN ROAD. Life and Literature Today. Part Three.
   Compiled by Andrew Scotland M.A. Ph.D. Nisbet. Contains:
   A Memory, p. 95, from G. K.'s Weekly (15 June 1935).

### 1939
*409Z. DETECTION MEDLEY. Edited by John Rhode. Hutchin-
   son. (n.d.) Contains: The Best Detective Story (pp. 106–7).

G. K. Chesterton was the first President of the Detection Club founded by Anthony Berkeley in 1929. Its members included the leading detective-story writers of the day. They contributed 'not cash, but the products of their industry' to defray the expenses of the Club. Publications:

1931. *The Floating Admiral* (377)

1933. *Ask a Policeman* (no contribution by G. K. C.)

1936. *The Anatomy of Murder* (no contribution by G. K. C.)

1939. *Detection Medley*. The Foreword to this volume, by John Rhode, gives a brief account of the Detection Club, refers to the death of G. K. Chesterton and to the election of E. C. Bentley as his successor as President. *The Best Detective Story* is reprinted from *G. K.'s Weekly*, 24 May 1934. (See also Maisie Ward: *Gilbert Keith Chesterton*. (782). pp. 466–8.)

### 1953

*413A. A SOCIALIST ANTHOLOGY and the Men Who Made It. Compiled with an historical introduction by Norman Longmate. Phoenix House. Contains: *Bear One Another's Burdens* (p. 150) from the unpublished Notebooks (*c.* 1895) quoted in Maisie Ward; *Gilbert Keith Chesterton* (782).

### 1960

*415. A PARTRIDGE IN A PEAR TREE. A Celebration for Christmas. Arranged by Neville Braybrooke. Darton, Longman and Todd. Contains: *Frances Xmas* 1900 (567).

### 1962

*416. PLATFORM AND PULPIT. Bernard Shaw. Edited with an introduction by Dan H. Laurence. Hart-Davies. Contains:

*Shaw versus Chesterton* (pp. 88–93). A debate in the Memorial Hall, London, 30 November 1911. Collected from *The Christian Commonwealth*, 6 and 13 December 1911.

*The Menace of the Leisured Woman* (pp. 168–71). A summation by Shaw, from the Chair, of a debate between G. K. Chesterton and Lady Rhondda, Kingsway Hall, 27 January 1927. Collected from *Time and Tide* 4 February 1927.

Also, pp. 98–9, the Shaw-Belloc debate in which Shaw made the famous reference to Chesterton as 'that large and flourishing intellectual property' under the control of Cadbury. In the same year (1913) Chesterton ceased to contribute to the Cadbury newspaper, the *Daily News*, which he had adorned since 1901.

# C

## PERIODICALS CONTAINING
## CONTRIBUTIONS BY G. K. CHESTERTON

### 501. ACADEMY

*For* 'July' *read* 'June'.

### *503A. AYLESFORD REVIEW

1967. Autumn. The Disaster of Europe. (Written *c.* 1923; hitherto unpublished. 'The original signed typescript, with holograph corrections, was given by Mr Chesterton to the late Father Walker, then parish priest of High Wycombe, and by Father Walker to Mr Hall', Editorial Note.)

### *504A. BLACKFRIARS

1922. October, Vol. III, No. 31. *Where All Roads Lead*: The Youth of the Church, I. November, No. 32. The Youth of the Church, II. December, No. 33. The Case for Complexity.

1923. January, No. 34. The History of a Half-truth, I. February, No. 35. The History of a Half-truth, II. March, No. 36. A Note on Comparative Religion, I. April, No. 37. A Note on Comparative Religion, II.

The pamphlet, *Where All Roads Lead* (113) is based on these essays.

### 509. CATHOLIC HERALD

*Add*, immediately below heading:

'1939. 15 December. True Sympathy: or Prevention of Cruelty to Teachers.'

First line of entry. For '1946 Sept. 27' *read* '1940 Sept. 27' and at end of this line add:

'First printed in *G. K.'s Weekly* 26 March 1936 and here reprinted on the occasion of the quatercentenary of the founding of the Jesuit Order. A note accompanying the poem in the *Catholic Herald* reads: "This must have been the latest, perhaps

the very last, work to come from the pen of G. K. Chesterton.
. . . The draft text, in his own writing, was found on his desk
after his final illness. It is clearly unfinished. But fortunately he
had already dictated his poem to Miss Collins, his secretary,
who, after his death, fulfilled his wish by forwarding the MS
and corrected text to Campion Hall, the Jesuit House of
Studies at Oxford where they are preserved in honour".'

At end of entry, *add*:

'1962. 28 December. Ballade of an Old Man. In facsimile holograph with two sketches.'


509A.  CHRISTMAS SPIRIT

*For* 'Fantastic' *read* 'Fanatic'.


517.  DAILY NEWS

1901.

*After* 'The Mistake about Stevenson (4)' *add*: '2 July. The
Poetry of Cities (112)' and *delete* the next word, 'July'.
*After* '. . . Don Quixote (110)' *add*: '5. The Library of the
Nursery (112). 11. Lunacy and Letters (112).'
*After* '. . . Tolstoy (4)' *add*: '7 November. The Everlasting
Nights (114). 15. The Meaning of Dreams (112).'
*After* '(4. Charlotte Brontë)' *add*: '13. A Wild Reconstruction
(112).'

1902.

*After* '1902' *add*: '8 January. The Meaning of the Theatre.
(112). 8 February. As Large as Life in Dickens (114).' and *delete*
the next word 'Feb.'.
*After* '(4. Pope and the Art of Satire)' *add*: '26 September. A
Defence of Bores (112). 30 October. A Neglected Originality
(112).'

1904.

*After* '1904' *add*: '2 January. January One (112).'
*After* 'Some Policemen and a Moral (16)' *add*: '18 June. The
Pessimist and the Door-Knocker (112).'
*After* 'Mr. Crowley and the Creeds (215)' *add*: '15 October.
Convention and the Hero (112).'

1905.

*Between* 'Dec.' and '25' *add*: '9. The Way to the Stars (112).'

1906.

*After* 'What I found in my Pocket (16)' *add*: '31. On Fragments (114).'

*Page* 126.

*After* 'Advantages of Having One Leg (234, 16)' *add*: '1 September. A Charge of Irreverence (112). 22. A Fairy Tale (112).'

*After* 'In Topsy-Turvy Land (16)' *add*: '12. The Paradox of Humility (112).'

1910.

*Between* 'April' and '16' *add*: '2. The Comic Constable (114).'

1911. (*Page* 127).

*After* '(28. The Architect of Spears)' *add*: '20. The Mirror (112).'

*After* '(28. The Wrong Incendiary)' *add*: '8. The Peasant (114).'

## 519. DEBATER

Page 130. Line 1. *For* 'No. 17. Nov.' *read* 'No. 17. Oct.'.

Mr Garry Wills, in *Chesterton, Man and Mask* (Sheed and Ward, New York, 1961), observes that Chesterton's contributions to the pseudonymous correspondence, *Letters of Three Friends*, are not listed in the bibliography. I now make good this omission and complete the *Debater* record by listing the other contributions by Chesterton not already recorded.

This schoolboy work, most of which has not been reprinted, is interesting for the light it throws upon Chesterton's development at this time, as Mr Wills demonstrates in his book.

*The Letters of Three Friends*

The exchange of letters runs through Volume III of the *Debater*, from March 1892 to February 1893. An editorial note states:

The three characters writing them are Guy Crawford, an artist of strong socialist tendencies; Lawrence Ormond, a London journalist of very little but personal tendencies; and E. Cusack Bremmil, a barrister, unfortunately of briefless tendencies.

The pseudonyms preserve the initials of their originals: Gilbert Chesterton, Lucian Oldershaw and E. Clerihew Bentley. Chesterton, as Guy Crawford, contributed the following: Vol.

III, No. 13, March 1892, Letter II from Guy Crawford Esq., the Florentine Gallery, Florence, to Lawrence Ormond Esq., Inner Temple. No. 14, May, G. C. to E. Cusack Bremmil, Inner Temple. No. 16, September, To E. C. B. No. 17, October, G. C., St Petersburg to L. O., Inner Temple. No. 18, February 1893. G. C., Inner Temple, to L. O., Nice.

### Great English Poets

A series of sixteen essays on the poets ran through all three volumes. They were unsigned but in the last issue, the Editor (Lucian Oldershaw) revealed that seven were by himself and the remaining nine by the Chairman of the J.D.C. (G. K. C.). The nine essays by Chesterton were: Vol. II, No. 3, May 1891, II, Milton. No. 6, August, VI, Gray. No. 7, September, VII, Cowper. No. 8, October, VIII, Burns. No. 9, November, IX, Wordsworth. No. 12, February 1892, XII, Scott. No. 14, May, XIV, Shelley. No. 15, July, XV, Browning.

### The White Cockade

A serial story, presented anonymously in the magazine but attributed to the Chairman in the Index.
Vol. II, No. 3, May 1891, *The White Cockade*, Chapter I, The Student; Chapter II, The Chevalier. No. 4, June, Chapter III, The Temptation. No. 5, July, Chapter IV, The Marquis. No. 6, August, Chapter V, The Arrest; The End.

### The Modern Novelist

Vol. III, No. 17, October 1892, *The Modern Novelist*, I, The Shooting of Blunam Lowne. By R— K—. No. 18, February 1893, II, Eric Gorston. By G— M—.
The demise of *The Debater* cut short this promising series of parodies.

---

*Opposite*

8. 'Humanity'. Written about 1892. Published in the *Debater*.

# Humanity

A poet, pallid and perverse  
  With witless love a watery curse.  
Rose up to Heaven with hosts sublime  
Of the insatiable time.  
He rent the angels' cohorts through  
And broke Heaven's blazonry of blue.  
And ever more he cries "What boon  
Can Jesus give, who was a man?"  
The last red guard was fighting still  
  Against the jeering Prince of Nil  
And as he rushed across the fray  
The insulted lord of star & spray  
Lifted his head "Thou sayest true;  
"I was a man: but what are you."

*G. K. Chesterton*

523. EVERYMAN

*Add*, as first entry:
'1912. October 18, Vol. I, No. 1, The Chance of the Peasant.
November 8, No. 4 (The Chance of the Peasant, A Rejoinder.
By F. McL.). November 22, No. 6, The Collapse of Socialism.
(A reply to F. McL.). December 6, No. 8 (The Alleged Col-
lapse of Socialism, Part I. By Bernard Shaw). December 13,
No. 9 (The Alleged Collapse of Socialism, Part II. By Bernard
Shaw). December 20, No. 10. A Salute to the Last Socialist.
(A Reply to Bernard Shaw.)'

526. G. K.'s WEEKLY

1925. (Page 132)
*After* 'Oct. 17. How to Write a Detective Story' *add*: '(114).'
1926
*After* 'March 27. Jealousy (69)' *add*: 'June 5. The Real Issue (114).'
1934. (Page 134)
*Add*: 'May 24. The Best Detective Story (409z).'
1935
*After* 'Killing the Nerve (97)' *add*: '30. Scipio and the Children
(114).'
1936
*Add*: Jan. 23. And So to Bed (114).
Last line of entry. After *'June 14]*' *add*: July 16. The Pipe of
Peace. Aug. 13. Detectives Real and Romantic.'

532. ILLUSTRATED LONDON NEWS

Page 135
*After* 'About Christianity. 17. viii. 35 (111).' *add*: 'About the
Workers. 20. vii. 35 (100).'
Page 136
*After* 'Creative and the Critical, On the. 11. iv. 31 (93).' *add*:
'Crime among the Teacups. 23. v. 36 (409x).'
Page 137
*After* 'King George V. 25. i. 36 (111)' *add*: 'King, On the. 6.
vii. 29 (86).'
Page 139
*After* 'S.T.C. 4. viii. 34 (100)' *add*: 'Sacredness of Sites, The. 11.
i. 30 (114).

534. JOHN O'LONDON'S WEEKLY
    At end of entry, *add*: '(114).'

*535A. LENDING LIBRARY AND BOOK BORROWER'S
    RECORD
    1934. Nov. Fiction as Food. (114).

536. LISTENER
    1933. (Page 143)
    *After* 'Evelyn M. Hatch' *add*: '(114)'.
    1934. (Page 144)
    *For* 'Dec. 26' *read* 'Dec. 27'.
    1936. (Page 145)
    *After* '*We Will End With a Bang*' *add*: '(114)'.

541. NATION
    *After* '1909' *add*: 'Nov. 11. On Imperialism. (A Letter.)'

541A. NEOLITH
    *Revise* entry to read:
    '1907. November. No. 1. The People of England. (The Secret
    People. 37.)'

*542A. NEW DAILY
    1906. Nov. 7. The Good Grocer. (An Apology.) (402.)

*542B. NEW ENGLISH WEEKLY
    1934. Nov. 15. A. R. Orage (408).

---

*Opposite*

9.  'The King'. Front page leader on the death of King George V,
published in *G. K.'s Weekly*, 23 January 1936.

# The King.

Today we salute sadly, but not only in sadness, a good man who was called to a great office. It is perhaps the heaviest criticism on our current culture, that ten thousand commentators will write as if the words "good" and "great" naturally go together. In truth, they are immortal antagonists. It is not easy for a man to be a good man: an echo of the empty modern cynicism can be awakened in its hollow caves of mere derision and despair, even by saying that he was a good husband or a good father. But it grows more difficult with every inch of enlargement: and to have an Empire to survey, and still be a good man, was perceived even by Marcus Aurelius to be a paradox. But degenerate Christianity has produced a decay in the perception of common things which was to paganism impossible: and even death and tragedy can now at last be vulgarised.

It is the returning might in the idea of Monarchy, that it presents in a single image that human simplicity which was attempted in the high vision of Democracy; and there betrayed by confusion and corruption. The perfect

**545. NEW WITNESS**

1914. (Page 148)
*After* 'May 7. The Higher Unity (37)' *add*: '21. On Holidays
(114).'
1919
*After* 'Songs of Education V (54)' *add*: 'Oct. 24. The Lost Railway Station (114).'
1921. (Page 149)
*Between* 'July' and '22' *add*: '15. The Soul in Every Legend
(114).'
1922
*After* 'At the Caxton Hall (Speech)' *add*: 'September 22. The
Camp and the Cathedral (114).'
*After* 'Dec. 1. Shakespeare and the Legal Lady (56)' *add*: '8.
Bethlehem and the Great Cities (114).'

**546. OBSERVER**

*Amend* second line to read:
'1920. June 6. Dickens 50 Years After (48).'
Third line. *For* 'April 14' *read* 'April 17'.

**★549A. OUT AND AWAY**

1919. July. Vol. I. No. 1. The End of the Roman Road (58).

**550. OUTLINE**

*Delete* '(341)' and *add*: 'Feb. 4. (Why I am not a Catholic. By
Canon Raven). Feb. 11. (The Enquiring Layman). March 31.
(The Logic of G. K. C. Examined).
1929. March 9. G. K. attacks the "New Religion". March 16.
(Plain Man replies.) April 13. Rejoinder by G. K. C. June 1
and 22 (The Silence of G. K. C.). June 29. The Case of Canon
Raven.'

**558. SPEAKER**

Line 4. *After* 'The Earth's Shame (2)' *add*: 'June 5. The Holy of
Holies (37).'
Lines 17–18. *After* 'July 27. The Last Hero (37)' *add*: 'Sentimental
Literature (114).'

565. T. P.'s WEEKLY
>   *Amend* third line to read:
>   '1910. April 29. Mark Twain (110).' *Add*: 'Christmas Number.
>   What is right with the World.
>   1911. April 7. Novel-Reading (114).'

567. TABLET
>   Third line. *Add*: '(415).'
>   At end of entry *add*:
>   '1955. June 18. Extract from *The Ballad of the White Horse* in
>   facsimile holograph.'

568. TIMES
>   First line. *Amend*, to read:
>   '1911. March 9. On Imperialism. (A letter to the *Nation* (541)
>   quoted in a libel action, Daily Express Ltd v. Penny Illustrated
>   Paper Ltd.)'

# D

# BOOKS AND PERIODICALS CONTAINING
# ILLUSTRATIONS BY G. K. CHESTERTON

## 1904

*606A. *The Idler.* June to December (monthly). Illustrations to the serialised version of *The Club of Queer Trades* (8 and 531).

## 1905

609.  *Biography for Beginners*
      *Add*:
      *The Origin of Biography for Beginners* (1893)
      The story of the invention of the clerihew by Edmund Clerihew Bentley and the first productions by himself and his friends at St Paul's School is told by E. C. Bentley in *Those Days* (Chapter V): 'I wrote a number . . . at a sitting one evening; and when G. K. C. and others got hold of the idea there came to be a large output among us. . . . They were written in a notebook, with sketches by G. K. C. . . . [which] turned up long afterwards in other hands. . . .'
      The notebook is now in the possession of St Paul's School and by courtesy of the High Master and the Librarian, I have examined it. Bound in green cloth with spine and corners black, it has attached to the inside back cover a typewritten note:

### NOTE

This is the original 'Dictionary of Biography'. The verses are in the handwriting of Edmund Clerihew Bentley and the illustrations are by Gilbert Keith Chesterton.
Although Bentley was the originator of the form—since known as the 'Clerihew'—and is the author of the great majority of the verses in this book, there were some collaborators.
Chesterton has indicated the authorship of each verse by pictorial signatures, the key to which is as follows:
The Dodo . . . Edmund Clerihew Bentley

The Gavel . . . Gilbert Keith Chesterton
The Stag's Head . . . L. R. F. Oldershaw
The Pipe . . . G. K. C.'s Father
The Double Pi . . . W. P. H. d'Avigdor
666 . . . Maurice Solomon
As will be seen, Bentley gave the book to me (Grey was my
nickname) and I rebound it in boards, the original brown
paper cover being bound in. This has altered the order of the
verses.

[*signed*] Maurice Solomon

The first page of the notebook has a dedicatory poem to
Maurice Solomon headed '666' and signed 'Edmund Clerihew
Bentley. Sept. 1893.' There follow two full-page drawings and
43 pages of biographies with many drawings in and around the
text and finally, two full-page drawings.
From the pictorial signatures it appears that G. K. C. wrote
the clerihews on Solomon, Jane Austen, Lawrence Sterne,
Doctor Parker, Cervantes, Thomas Carlyle and the Rev.
Stopford Brooke. He collaborated with Bentley in: Dean
Colet, Robert Burns, Lord Rosebery, William Cobbett, Saul,
Laurence Oliphant, Ruskin, Henry Irving, Savonarola,
Paderewski, and Ezekiel. J. H. Spurgeon, apparently, demanded
the combined talents of G. K. C., Bentley and d'Avigdor.
Of all of those in which G. K. C. had a hand, only Cervantes
and Jane Austen survive in *Biography for Beginners*.

### 1909

*609C. *Granta*. December. A drawing: *After the Bump Supper* (615A).

### 1922

614. *The Mercy of Allah*, by Hilaire Belloc.
> At end of entry, *add*: 'The dust jacket was later withdrawn by
> the publishers. (See Robert Speaight. *Life of Hilaire Belloc*. p.
> 474.)'

### 1924

615. *Stampede!* by L. de Giberne Sieveking.
> At end of entry, *add*: 'Frontispiece, one full-page and one
> double-page drawing in red crayon on tinted paper and four-
> teen line illustrations in the text. The double-page drawing is

reproduced on the dust-jacket. On p. (13), six lines of prose in facsimile holograph, signed, G. K. Chesterton.'

## 1929
622. *More Biography*, by E. Clerihew Bentley.
     At end of entry, *add*: 'The clerihews, with G. K. C.'s drawings, appeared in *Pall Mall Magazine* monthly from May to September 1929.'

## 1930
625. *G. K.'s Weekly*. Dec. 27.
     At end of entry, *add*: '(400)'.

## 1931
626. *G. K.'s Weekly*. Jan. 10.
     At end of entry, *add*: '(400)'.

*626A. *Mutt's Mutterings* 1931. The Official Organ and Christmas Annual of the Maidenhead Mutts. Cartoon: *Contribution by one who might be a Mutt but prefers to be a Mug. G. K. C.*

## 1941
643. *As it Happened*
     At end of entry, *add*: '(776)'.

## 1953
*647A. *The Saturday Book*. Edited by John Hadfield. A poem in holograph with illustration: *'Lo! Masterman and Chesterton.'* (p. 273).

## 1964
*650. *Theatre Notebook*. Summer. Plate 3. *Hiram Stead and Sir Henry Irving*, by G. K. Chesterton. The original (drawn *c*. 1905) is in the Harvard Theatre Collection.

# E

## BOOKS AND ARTICLES ABOUT
## G. K. CHESTERTON

### 1904

*702A.  Aleister Crowley. *Why Jesus Wept*. A Study of Society and the Grace of God. Privately Printed. (Philippe Renouard. Paris.) Has a *Dedicatio Extraordinaria* addressed to 'Dear Mr Chesterton' who makes a brief appearance in Scene XIII as 'a Provost of Queer Street'. (See 215.)

### 1909

708.  G. Bernard Shaw. Chesterton on Shaw.
For 'Aug. 25' *read* 'Aug. 28'.

### 1916

717.  G. Bernard Shaw. The Case against Chesterton.
For '(741)' *read* '(See 544 and 741)'.

*717A.  Dixon Scott. The Guilt of Mr Chesterton. In *Men of Letters*. Hodder and Stoughton.

### 1920

*721B.  Frank Harris. Gilbert K. Chesterton. In *Contemporary Portraits* (Third Series). New York. Published by the author.

### 1923

*727A.  St John Ervine. G. K. Chesterton. In *Some Impressions of My Elders*. Allen and Unwin.

729.  Arnold Lunn. 'Roman Converts'. A Reply to Mr Chesterton.
*Lower* this entry to below the heading '1925'.

### 1927

733.  J. C. Squire. Mr Chesterton's Verse.
At end of entry, *add*: '(739A)'.

*734A.  Willem Nieuwenhuis. *Chesterton*. Roermond. J. J. Romen en Zonen. A critical study, in Dutch.

## 1930

\*739A. J. C. Squire. Mr Chesterton's Verse. In *Sunday Mornings.* Heinemann.

## 1931

\*740A. Frederic Whyte. 'G. K. C.' In *A Bachelor's London.* Grant Richards.

## 1932

743. Ivor Brown. Bobbe-up-and-Doun.
 *For* 'April 7' *read* 'April 10'. *For* April 14' *read* 'April 17'.

\*743A. Desmond McCarthy. 'I Wonder at Not Wondering'. *Sunday Times.* 17 Sept. A review of *Collected Poems.* (G. K. C. replied in a letter, *Sunday Times,* 24 Sept.)

## 1936

749. *Obituary Notices.*
 Lines 5–6 of entry. *Delete* 'G. K. Chesterton. Portrait of a Friend. *American Review.* Oct.'
 Line 7. E. C. Bentley. *For* 'June 20' *read* 'June 17'.
 Page 166, line 6. After 'June 20' *add*: '(763A).'

## 1937

\*757A. Eric Gill. Review article on the *Autobiography. Dublin Review.* April.

\*763A. Robert Lynd ('Y.Y.'). *In Defence of Pink.* Dent.
 The first essay defends pink against G. K. C.'s attack on it in *As I Was Saying*; the last is the obituary article (749).

## 1938

766. D. de Pauw, O.P. *Gilbert Keith Chesterton.*
 *For* 'Standaard-Bockhandel' *read* 'Standaard-Boekhandel'.

## 1940

774. A. M. A. Bogaerts. *Chesterton and the Victorian Age.*
 *Delete* 'Translated . . . Dutch'.
 *After* 'Hilversum' *add*: 'Rozenbecken Venemans. Uitgevers-bedr. N.V.'

## 1941

777. Ronald Knox. G. K. Chesterton: the Man and his Work.
   At end of entry, *add*: '(822A)'.
780. Maisie Ward. . . .
   *Below* this entry *add*, as heading: '**1942**'
\*781A. Edward J. Macdonald. G. K. C.'s Last Days. *Universe.* 15 June.
\*781B. Douglas Woodruff. On Newman, Chesterton and Exorbitance.
   In *For Hilaire Belloc. Essays on his 72nd Birthday.* Edited by
   Douglas Woodruff. Sheed and Ward.

## 1943

782. Maisie Ward. *Gilbert Keith Chesterton.*
   For '(London 1945)' *read* '(London 1944)'.

## 1944

\*784A. Graham Greene. G. K. Chesterton. *Spectator.* April 21.

## 1945

\*792C. E. Verstraden, S. J. *G. K. Chesterton's Conversion.* Light of the
   East Series, No. 24. Ranchi. Catholic Press.

## 1946

797. James Stephens. The 'Period Talent'.
   For '(See 797)' *read* '(See 798)'.
798. C. S. Lewis. Notes on the Way.
   For '(796)' *read* '(797)'.

## 1952

812. Michael Asquith. G. K. Chesterton: Prophet. . . .
   At end of entry *add*: '(822A)'.

## 1955

\*822A. Richard Church (Ed.). *The Spoken Word.* Collins. Contains:
   G. K. Chesterton by Mgr Ronald Knox (777) and Chesterton by
   Michael Asquith (812).
\*822B. C. S. Lewis. *Surprised by Joy.* Geoffrey Bles.
   'In reading Chesterton . . . I did not know what I was letting
   myself in for. A young man who wishes to remain a sound
   Atheist cannot be too careful of his reading.'

## 1956

*825B. J. J. Sullivan. G. K. Chesterton. *Manchester Review*. Autumn.

## 1957

828. John Raymond. Jee Kaycee.
At end of entry *add*: '(833)'.
*830. Gustavo Corcao. *My Neighbour as Myself*. Translated from the Portuguese by Clotilde Wilson. Longmans. Chapter 17, Chesterton and Maritain.

## 1958

*831. Vincent Brome. *Six Studies in Quarrelling*. Cresset Press. Chapter 5, G. K. Chesterton *versus* Bernard Shaw.
*832. Robert Speaight (Ed.). *Letters from Hilaire Belloc*. Hollis and Carter.
*833. John Raymond. *England's on the Anvil*. Collins. Contains: Jee Kaycee (828).
*834. R. G. G. Price. Beginners' Slope, Check-up on Chesterton's Detective. *Punch*, July 23.
*835. R. A. Knox. *Literary Distractions*. Sheed and Ward. XII, G. K. Chesterton (752 re-titled). XIII, Father Brown. XIV, Detective Stories.

## 1959

*836. Bernard Bergonzi. Chesterton and/or Belloc. *Critical Quarterly*, Vol. I, No. 1, Spring.
*837. J. Gordon Eaker. G. K. Chesterton among the Moderns. *Georgia Review*, Vol. XIII, No. 2, Summer.
*838. Michael Mason. *The Centre of Hilarity*. Sheed and Ward.
A great part of this unusual and neglected book is devoted to a study of the contrast between the achievement of T. S. Eliot and that of G. K. Chesterton.
'The extent of the difference between these men, and the extent to which the intellectual climate of England has changed in the past quarter-century, is sufficiently illustrated by the fact that today many would consider it almost ludicrous to compare them. And whether or not you agree that Chesterton is unworthy of serious consideration in the same breath with Mr Eliot, or whatever the qualifications with which you accept

some part of that attitude, you can hardly deny that the contrast between them is extreme. Where Mr Eliot is austere,
Chesterton is genial; where Mr Eliot is desperately earnest,
Chesterton is scandalously playful; where Mr Eliot conveys a
painfully achieved approval of existence, Chesterton conveys
a childlike exultation in it; where Mr Eliot cultivates a pretty
Christian wit, Chesterton bubbles over with laughter. Viewed
in the light of humanism's increasingly stringent critique of
the culture and society it has created, the first appears as
essentially distinguished, the second as essentially vulgar. And
it is really in virtue of that culminating distinction between
"mass civilisation and minority culture" that we have to account for the fact that Chesterton is hardly taken seriously at
all by the intellectuals—the "clerks"—of the Second World
War period, or their successors of the atomic age. To the
majority of them, probably, there is no surer sign of his failure
to achieve membership of the cultural élite than his fundamental
happiness and pleasure in the being both of himself and everything else. Indeed, for many of the most sensitive and intelligent
men of today happiness of any basic kind is either escapism or
immaturity, and despair the very stuff of adulthood. It's hardly
surprising that for such Chesterton invites a critical placing so
easy as to involve little critical effort at all.'

*839. Evelyn Waugh. *Ronald Knox*. Chapman and Hall.
In Appendix II, pp. 207–8, a letter from Chesterton to Ronald
Knox is printed which had been omitted from the important
series of undated letters (written in the summer of 1922) given
in Maisie Ward's biography (782), pp. 391–5.

## 1960

*840. *Carroll Quarterly*, Vol. 13, Nos. 3–4, Spring–Summer. John
Carroll University, Cleveland, Ohio. *A Tribute to Chesterton*
and five articles on various aspects of his work.

## 1961

*841. Garry Wills. *Chesterton: Man and Mask*. New York. Sheed and
Ward.
A valuable critical work, based on extensive research.

*842. Edward J. Macdonald. Chesterton—genius inspired by his faith.
*Universe*, June 9.

*843. Clare Nicholl. The Way to a Friend's House is Never Far. *Catholic Herald*, June 9.

The above two entries relate to the twenty-fifth anniversary of the death of Chesterton.

## 1962

*844. Neville Braybrooke. The Poet of Fleet Street. *John O'London's*, Feb. 8. No. 17 in the series 'Great Writers'.

*845. John Wain remembers how he was enthralled by *Manalive* by G. K. Chesterton. *Punch*, April 4. In the series 'Good Bad Books'.

*846. Garry Wills. The Secret Festival (A Chesterton Anniversary). *Catholic Book Reporter*. U.S.A. April–May.
'Must we wait, then, for a growth in understanding to supply warmth of remembrance? No. There is no need to "work up" a Chesterton vogue or revival. The kind of festivity he would want goes on, apart from all critical acclaim or eclipse.'

*847. Hesketh Pearson. Gilbert Keith Chesterton. In *Lives of the Wits*. pp. 302–18. Heinemann.

*848. Bernard Shaw. How Ireland Impressed Mr Chesterton. In *The Matter with Ireland*. Edited with an Introduction by David H. Greene and Dan H. Laurence. This review of *Irish Impressions* is collected from *The Irish Statesman*, Nov. 22 1919. 'The world is not half thankful enough for Chesterton; and I hope Ireland will not be among the ingrates; for no Irishman alive or dead has ever served her better and more faithfully with a pen than he.'

## 1963

*849. Malcolm Muggeridge. G. K. C. *New Statesman,* 23 August.
'He felt a deep, instinctive distaste for the way the 20th century was going which enabled him, in his early years of pessimism, to be an impressive prophet. "The earnest Freethinkers", he wrote in 1905, "need not worry themselves so much about the persecutions of the past. Before the Liberal idea is dead or triumphant, we shall see wars and persecutions the like of which the world has never seen." Stalin, then a young man of 26, and Hitler, 10 years younger, were, along with others, to make good his words to a fabulous degree.

It is surprising, in a way, that, when Chesterton was so often proved right in his judgments, he should still be less seriously regarded than contemporaries like Wells and the Webbs who were almost invariably wrong.'

*850. H. A. King. Living with Chesterton. *The Converts' Aid Society Annual Report*, 1963.

## 1964

*850A. Leo Anthony Hetzler. *The Early Literary Career of G. K. Chesterton: his literary apprenticeship and an analysis of his thought*, 1874–1914. Cornell University Ph.D. thesis. University Microfilms Inc., Ann Arbor, Michigan.

*850B. Rudolf Matthias Fabritius. *Das Komische im Erzählwerk G. K. Chestertons*. Max Niemeyer. Tubingen.

## 1966

*850C. Christopher Hollis. G. K. Chesterton. *New Knowledge*, Vol. 8, No. 12 (undated).

## COLLECTIONS AND SELECTIONS

### 1927

857. THE MINERVA EDITION
Second line of entry: *For* 'Nine' *read* 'Eleven'.
Third line: *Delete* 'all . . . Methuen'.
Last line: *Replace* full stop after '*Diversity*' by a comma and *add*:
'*Heretics, Orthodoxy.*'

### 1935

865. STORIES, ESSAYS AND POEMS. *Everyman.* An introduction by Maisie Ward was added in 1957.

### 1936

866. G. K. CHESTERTON OMNIBUS
First published in 1932, *not* in 1936.

### 1958

*875. THE FIRST BOOK OF FATHER BROWN. G. K.
Chesterton. Edited by Andrew Scotland M.A., Ph.D. Cassell.
Silver Circle Readers. Three stories from *The Innocence of
Father Brown* (*The Blue Cross, The Invisible Man*, and *The
Flying Stars*) edited for schools. In the same series:

THE SECOND BOOK OF FATHER BROWN (*The
Absence of Mr Glass* and *The Salad of Colonel Gray* from *The
Wisdom of Father Brown*; and *The Queer Feet* from *The Innocence
of Father Brown*).

THE THIRD BOOK OF FATHER BROWN (*The God
of the Gongs* from *The Wisdom of Father Brown*; *The Mirror of
the Magistrate* from *The Secret of Father Brown*; and *The Three
Tools of Death* from *The Innocence of Father Brown*).

THE FOURTH BOOK OF FATHER BROWN (*The
Insoluble Problem* and *The Blast of the Book* from *The Scandal of
Father Brown*; and *The Paradise of Thieves* from *The Wisdom
of Father Brown*).

*876. ESSAYS AND POEMS. A selection of Chesterton's articles
and poems on many controversial themes. Edited by Wilfred
Sheed. Penguin Books.

### 1959

*877. G. K. CHESTERTON. FATHER BROWN STORIES.
Illustrations by Edward Ardizzone. Folio Society.
Fourteen stories from the five Father Brown books, with
fourteen full-page illustrations.

### 1960–8

*878. REPRINT SERIES. *I. The Club of Queer Trades.* Darwen
Finlayson. 1960. *II. The Man Who Knew Too Much.* 1961.
*III. Manalive. IV. Four Faultless Felons. V. The Poet and the
Lunatics. VI. Tales of the Long Bow.* 1962. *VII. The Return of
Don Quixote. VIII. The Paradoxes of Mr Pond. IX. The Ball
and the Cross. X. The Man Who Was Thursday.* 1963. *XI. The
Napoleon of Notting Hill.* 1964. *XII. Tremendous Trifles.* 1968.
The last four volumes in this series were published, appropri-
ately enough, in Beaconsfield.

### 1964

*879. THE MAN WHO WAS ORTHODOX. A selection from
the Uncollected Writings of G. K. Chesterton. Arranged and
Introduced by A. L. Maycock. Dennis Dobson. A selection
from Chesterton's uncollected journalism prefaced by a long
and valuable critical introduction.

# G

## TRANSLATIONS INTO FOREIGN LANGUAGES
## OF BOOKS BY G. K. CHESTERTON

901. *CZECHOSLOVAKIAN*

**1960**

★ *Příběhy otce Browna.* J. Z. Novák. Preface by J. Hornát. Prague, Státni Nakladatelstiv Krasné Literatury, Hudby a Umeni. (Thirteen Father Brown stories.)

902. *DANISH*

**1959**

★ *Frit Nkeri og Rettroenhed* (*Orthodoxy*) H. Kehler. Copenhagen, Frimodt.

**1960**

*Manden som var Torsdag* (*The Man Who Was Thursday*). J. Ewald. Thaning and Appel.

903. *DUTCH*

**1910**

★ *Orthodoxie.* P. Kerstens. The Hague, M. Hols.

**1915**

★ *Berlijnsche Barbaarschneid.* (*The Barbarism of Berlin.*) W. de Veer. London, Nelson. (n.d.)

★ *Brieven aan een oud-Garibaldiaan.* (*Letters to an Old Garibaldian.*) W. de Veer. London. (n.d.)

**1917**

★ *Lord Kitchener.* Amsterdam, Ellerman, Harms. (n.d.)

★ *Avonturen van Father Brown.* W. Nieuwenhuis. Bossum, Paul Brand.

★ *Tooverij; een fantastisch blijspel.* (*Magic.*) S. B. Stokvis. Amsterdam, van Holkema and Warendorff.

**1920**

★    *Wie is Donderdag?* (*The Man Who Was Thursday*.) W. Steenhoff. Leiden, Uitgevers Mij. Futura.

**1923**

★    *Ketterij en Orthodoxie*. (Extracts from *Heretics* and *Orthodoxy*.) Fr Dupont and Fr Haepers. Louvain, Ghent, Malines, De Vlaamsche Boekanhalle.

**1924**

★    *S. Franciscus van Assisi*. W. Moens. 's Gravenhage, B. Mensing.

**1925**

*Amend* entry to read:
*Het bijgeloof der echtscheiding*. (*The Superstition of Divorce*.) P. Kerstens. Amsterdam, Uitg. 'Joost van den Vondel'.

**1926**

*Delete* first entry.
*Amend* second entry to read:
*De eeuwige mensch*. (*The Everlasting Man*.) H. Reijnen. Maastricht, Gebr. van Aelst. Second (revised) edition, Utrecht, Het Spectrum, 1948.

**1927**

*Amend* entry to read:
*Kerk en Bekeering*. (*The Catholic Church and Conversion*.) E. Russe. Voorhout, Foreholte.
★    *De Krankzinnige rechter*. (*The Club of Queer Trades*.) F. van Velsen. Tilburg, Het Nederlandsche Boekhuis. Second (revised) edition, 1949.

**1929**

★    *The Innocence of Father Brown*. N. H. M. Zwager. Groningen, J. B. Wolters. (Edited for schools.)
★    *De Vliegende Herberg*. (*The Flying Inn*.) J. H. P. Jacobs. Tilburg, Het Nederlandsche Boekhuis.
★    *Het eeuwig twistgesprek*. (*The Ball and the Cross*.) C. Hendriks. Hilversum, Paul Brand.

**1934**

★ *De Heilige Thomas van Aquino. (St Thomas Aquinas.)* H. Reijnen. Voorhout, Uitg. Foreholte.

**1937**

★ *De geschiedenis van mijn leven. (Autobiography.)* J. Panhuysen. Voorhout, Uitg. Foreholte.

**1938**

★ *Wat mankeert de wereld? (What's Wrong with the World.)* J. Panhuysen. Heemstede, De Toorts.

**1947**

*Add,* after 'D. Houtman'; 'Nijmegen, De Koepel.'.

**1951**

★ *Avonturen van Father Brown. (The Father Brown Stories.)* Two volumes. G. Bomans *et al.* Bossum, Paul Brand. Antwerp, Sheed and Ward.

**1953**

*Amend* title to read: *De Man die Te Veel Wist.*

**1954.**

*Delete* entry.

**1958**

★ *Father Brown Hondt Zich Van den Domme. (The Innocence of Father Brown.)* A. A. O. Arens, A.F.C. Brosens *et al.* Antwerp, Het Spectrum.

**1960**

★ *De Wijsheid van Father Brown. (The Widsom of Father Brown.)* E. Brongersma and A. Norbeck. Antwerp. Prisma-Boeken.

905. *FRENCH*

**1914**

First line of entry. *For* 'Garabaldien' *read* 'Garibaldien'.

**1922**

★    Petite Histoire d'Angleterre. A. Osmont. Paris, G. Crès.

**1925**

★    *Saint François d'Assise*. I. Rivière. Paris, Plon.

**1926**

★    *La Nouvelle Jérusalem*. J. Fournier-Pargoire. Paris, Perrin.

**1927**

After the entry *add*:
A translation of Part I of *The Everlasting Man*. (See below under 1947.)

**1928**

*For* 'Blond' *read* 'Bloud'.

**1929**

★    *La Vie de William Cobbett*. M. Agobert. Paris, Gallimard.
*Le Secret du Père Brown*. Mme F. Maury. Paris, Gallimard.

**1930**

*Delete* first, third and fifth lines.

**1934**

*Delete* whole entry.

**1936**

★    *L'amiral flottant* (377). Delvine. Paris, N.R.F.

**1937**

★    *Le Club des Métiers Bizarres*. (*The Club of Queer Trades*.) Saint Clair-Gray. Paris, N.R.F.

**1946**

★    *Le défenseur*. G. A. Garnier. Fribourg, Librairie de l'Université.

**1947**

★   *L'Homme Qu'on Appelle le Christ.* L. M. Gautier. Paris, Nouvelles Editions Latines.
A translation of Part II of *The Everlasting Man* with a long introduction by the translator and a bibliography of translations of Chesterton into French.

**1948**

★   *L'Homme à la Clef d'Or.* (*Autobiography.*) M. Beerblock. Brussels, Desclée de Brouwer.
With an introduction, chronology, bibliography, 88 pages of notes, a cartoon of the Chesterbelloc by Thomas Derrick and three drawings by Chesterton (two from *The Coloured Lands* and one from an unidentified source—'Signing a cheque. 1912').

**1952**

*L'église catholique et la Conversion.* R. Aouad. Paris, Bonne Presse.

906. *GAELIC*

Above entry, *add*: '**1937**'.
Second line, *delete*: '(n.d.)'.

907. *GERMAN*

**1909**

★   *Orthodoxie.* F. Blie. Munich, H. von Weber.

**1912**

★   *Häretiker.* Munich. G. Müller.

**1913**

*Priester und Detektiv.* (*The Innocence of Father Brown.*) H. M. von Lama. Regensburg, Kösel.

**1916**

★   *Dickens.* H. E. Herlitcska. Vienna, Phaidon.

**1917**

★   *Verteidigung des Unsinns.* (*The Defendant.*) Leipzig and Munich, Musarion.

**1922**

★   *Das Fliegende Wirtshaus.* (*The Flying Inn.*) J. Grabisch. Munich, Musarion.

**1924**

*Amend* line 1 to read:
*Was unrecht ist an der Welt.* (*What's Wrong with the World.*)
C. Meitner. Munich, Musarion.
*Delete* lines 2 and 3.

**1925**

*Amend* entry to read:
*Der Mann, der zuviel wusste.* (*The Man Who Knew Too Much.*)
C. Meitner. Munich, Musarion.
★   *G. B. Shaw.* C. Meitner and L. Goldscheider. Vienna, Phaidon.

**1926**

*Delete* both entries and *add*:
*Menschenkind!* (*Manalive.*) E. McCalman and N. Collins.
Munich, Musarion.

**1927**

*Amend* second entry to read:
'*Der hl. Franziskus von Assisi.* (*St Francis of Assisi.*) J. Benvenisti. Munich, Kasel.'
★   *Des Paradies der Diebe.* (*The Wisdom of Father Brown.*) C. Meitner. Munich, Musarion.
★   *Der Held von Notting Hill.* (*The Napoleon of Notting Hill.*) M. Georg. Bremen, Schunemann.
★   *Die verdachtigen Schritte.* (*The Innocence of Father Brown.*) H. M. von Lama. Munich, Kasel.
★   *Don Quijotes Wiederkehr.* (*The Return of Don Quixote.*) C. Thesing. Bremen, Schunemann.

**1928**

★   *Der geheimnisvolle Klub.* (*The Club of Queer Trades.*) R. Nutt. Munich, Musarion.

### 1929
*Delete* entry.

### 1930
*Amend* first entry to read:
*Ein Streitgespräch zwischen G.B.S. und G.K.C. (Do We Agree?)*
F. Lindemann. Bremen, Schunemann.
*Amend* second entry to read:
*Das neue Jerusalem. (The New Jerusalem.)* C. Thesing. Bremen,
Schunemann.
*Amend* third entry to read:
*Der unsterbliche Mensch. (The Everlasting Man.)* C. Thesing.
Bremen, Schunemann.

### 1933
*Delete* entry.

### 1935
★  *Der hl. Thomas von Aquin. (St Thomas Aquinas.)* E. Kaufmann.
Salzburg, Pustet.

### 1936
*Delete* entry.

### 1937
*Delete* second entry.

### 1945
*Delete* entry.

### 1947
★  *Bernard Shaw.* A. Sellner. Vienna, Amandus. (A translation into
German of the chapter on Shaw in *Heretics.*)

### 1949
★  *Aphorismen und paradoxa.* Selected by F. Simeth. Introduction
by F. Knapp. Donauworth, Verlag Cassianeum.

**1958**

★     *Der Spiegel.* (Thirteen essays from *Lunacy and Letters*.) J. Piron. Munich, Langen and Muller.
*Das Geheimnis des Pater Brown.* (*The Secret of Father Brown*.) A. P. Zeller. Munich, Droemer.

**1963**

★     *Ballspiel Mit Ideen.* (Thirty-five essays from seven books. With an introduction and epilogue by the translator.) M. Mullerott. Freiburg, Herder.

★ 907A.  *HEBREW*

**1960**

*The Innocence of Father Brown.*

908. *HUNGARIAN*

**1958**

★     *A Jambor Brown Atya.* (*The Innocence of Father Brown*.) T. Bartos. Budapest, Europa.

909. *ITALIAN*

**1956**

★     *Opera Scelte.* (*The Man Who Was Thursday, The Ball and the Cross, Manalive,* and twenty Father Brown stories.) E. Cecchi, M. Bartolliotti *et al.*

**1957**

★     *L'Uomo che fu Giovedi.* (*The Man Who Was Thursday*.) B. B. Serra. Milan, Rizzoli.

**1962**

★     *Saggi Scelti.* A cura di Dorothy Collins. (*Selected Essays.* 870.) F. Ballini. Alba, Paoline.

910. *JAPANESE*

**1958**

★     *The Incredulity of Father Brown.* Toshiro Murasaki. Tokyo, Hayakawa shobô.

**1959**

★ *The Secret of Father Brown.* Toshiro Murasaki. Tokyo, Hayakawa shobô.

★ *The Scandal of Father Brown.* Toshiro Murasaki. Tokyo, Hayakawa shobô.

★ *The Poet and the Lunatics.* T. Fukuda. Tokyo, Sôgen-sha.

**1960**

★ *The Club of Queer Trades.* T. Fukuda. Tokyo, Sôgen-sha.

**1961**

★ *The Paradoxes of Mr Pond.* T. Fukuda. Tokyo, Sôgen-sha.

## 912. *POLISH*

**1948**

*Amend* entry to read:
*Manalive.* Zygmunt Jakimiak. Warsaw, Pax.

**1955**

*Delete* entry.

**1959**

★ *Napoleon Z Notting Hill.* J. Laszczowa. Warsaw, Pax.

**1960**

★ *Latajaca Gospoda.* (*The Flying Inn.*) H. Oledzka. Warsaw, Pax.
*Przygody Ksiedza Brown.* (*The Father Brown Stories.*) T. J. Dehnel. Warsaw, Pax.

**1961**

★ *Swiety Franciszek Z Asyzu.* (*St Francis of Assisi.*) A. Chojecki. Warsaw, Pax.

★ *Swiety Tomasz Z Akwinu.* (*St Thomas Aquinas.*) A. Chojecki. Warsaw, Pax.

## 913. *PORTUGUESE*

**1958**

★ *Disparatos do Mundo.* (*What's Wrong with the World.*) J. Blanc de Portugal. Lisbon, Livraria Morais.

C.C. B.S.—7

**1959**

★   *A Estalageon Volante.* (*The Flying Inn.*) J. C. Beckert d'Assump-
cao. Lisbon, Editorial Aster.

## 914. RUSSIAN

**1958**

★   *The Incredulity of Father Brown.* E. Roks. Tallin, Estgosizdat.
G. K. Chesterton. *Stories.* (Fifteen Father Brown stories.)
Translation edited by A. Gavrilova. Foreword by A. Yelis-
tratova. Moscow, State Publishing House.

## 915. SPANISH

**1956**

*Amend* entry to read:
'*Father Brown Stories.* (The twelve stories in *The Wisdom of
Father Brown* issued separately in a uniform edition, 1956 and
later.) Maria Antonia Oyuela de Grant. Buenos Aires, Editorial
La Isla.'

★   *Cuatro Pillos.* (*Four Faultless Felons.*) Mexico, Novarro.

**1958**

★   *El Hombre Commun.* (*The Common Man.*) A. Franco. Buenos
Aires, Editorial Heroica.

**1959**

★   *El Reverso de la Locura.* (*Lunacy and Letters.*) G. Blanco. San-
tiago, Editorial del Nuevo Extremo.

★   *La Paradoja Andante y Otras Essayos.* (*The Glass Walking Stick.*)
L. Echavarri. Buenos Aires.

## 916. SWEDISH

**1959**

★   *Mannem som var Torsdag.* (*The Man Who Was Thursday.*)
M. L. Elliott. Stockholm, Natur O Kultur.

**1965**

★   *Den Oöverträffade fader Brown.* (Eleven Father Brown stories
from three books.) P. Beckman. Stockholm, Tidens Bokklubb.

# H

## G. K. C. MISCELLANY

951. (*c*) *Caricatures*

In '(ii) By Max Beerbohm', *add*:

'1925. *The Old and the Young Self: Mr G. K. Chesterton.* Both the above are reproduced in *Caricatures by Max. From the Collection in the Ashmolean Museum.* O.U.P. 1958.'

(iii) By David Low.

Immediately after 'Lynx' *add*: '(Rebecca West).

This caricature is also reproduced in *Ye Madde Designer*, by Low (*The Studio*, 1935) with an interesting account (pp. 47–8) of how it was composed.'


953. *Miscellaneous*

*Add*:

(ii)a. 1932. Bernard Shaw. *Short Stories, Scraps and Shavings.* Constable. Contains: A Glimpse of the Domesticity of Franklin Barnabas, a discarded fragment of *Back to Methuselah.* 'There can be no doubt at all that G. K. Chesterton was the original of Immenso Champernoon, the voluble punster, "a man of colossal mould with the head of a cherub on the body of a Falstaff".'

A broadcast performance of this piece was given on 28 July 1958.

*Add*:

(iii)a. 1936. *The Donkey.* For chorus of Men's Voices (unaccompanied). Music by Hugh S. Robertson. Curwen.

*Amend* '(iii)' to read '(iii)b.'

*Add*:

(iii)c. 1945. *Hymn of Dedication* (G. K. Chesterton). For chorus and orchestra. Music by William Wordsworth. Alfred Lengnick.

*Add*:

(iii)d. 1947. *The Donkey.* By G. K. Chesterton. For medium voice and piano. Music by Henry Cowell. New York. Music Press.

*Add*:

(iii)e. 1954. *Old Noah*. Song. Words by G. K. Chesterton. Music by Joseph Batten. Boosey and Hawkes.

*Add*:

(v). 1962. Frances Donaldson. *The Marconi Scandal*. Hart-Davis.

954. *Memorials*

(ii) *Amend* inscription to read:

'Gilbert Keith Chesterton 1874–1936
poet, novelist and critic
lived here'

*Add*:

(v). 1960. (Marie Lamigeon.) *Church of S. Teresa of the Child Jesus and SS. Thomas More and John Fisher*. Beaconsfield. Challoner Publications.

A short illustrated history of the parish of Beaconsfield with an account of the building of the Catholic Church which was completed as a memorial to G. K. Chesterton. Contains (pp. 17–22) *Gilbert Keith Chesterton. b. 1874. d. 1936. An illustrious parishioner of St. Teresa's Church, Beaconsfield* by the Very Reverend Canon C. M. Davidson D.D. B.A. R.D.

(vi). 1967. Plaque on Top Meadow, Beaconsfield. Inscribed:

G. K. Chesterton
Lived here
1922–1936

Beaconsfield and District Historical
Society. Erected by Dorothy E. Collins.

# CHESTERTON CONTINUED

A selection of prose and verse by G. K. Chesterton, spanning his writing life, 1900–36 and now first collected.

> *Frances: Xmas* 1900
> *Sorrow* (from the French of Charles Guérin) A prizewinning poem 1908
> Criticism of *Magic* 1914
> Three letters to E. V. Lucas 1917–26
> *Dickens and Christmas.* A broadcast to the U.S.A. 1931
> *Ballade of a Morbid Modern* 1933
> *The Good Grocer* 1935
> *Comfort for Communists* 1935
> *True Sympathy* (n.d.)
> *To the Jesuits* (*Spain,* 1936)

# FRANCES: XMAS 1900

[This poem was written on the fly-leaf of *The Wild Knight* (2) which was published the year before Chesterton's marriage. It was not included in *Collected Poems* but was printed in facsimile in the *Tablet* (567), 15 June 1946 and in *A Partridge in a Pear Tree* (415) in 1960.]

Dearest: whatever others see
Herein, it is no mystery—
That I find all the world is good
Since you are all the world to me.

You will not blame my boastful hours,
It is not of such souls as yours
To spew the wrath of sorrow out
Upon the harmless grass and flowers.

Do you fight on for all the press,
Wise as you are, you cannot guess
How I shall flaunt before God's Knights
The triumph of my own princess.

Almost this day of the strange star
We know the bonfire old and far
Whence all the stars as sparks are blown
Piled up to warm us after war.

There when we spread our hands like wings,
And tell good tales of conquered things
The tale that I shall tell of you
Shall clash the cups of all the Kings.

I swear it shall be mine alone
To tell your tale before the throne
To tell your tale beside the fire
Eternal. Here I tell my own.

# SORROW

*(From the French of Charles Guérin)*

[A prize-winning poem in a *Westminster Gazette* literary competition.
It was published in the *Westminster Gazette* (573) 24 October 1908 and
in *The Second Problems Book. Prizes and Proximes from the Westminster
Gazette*, 1908–9 (250A).]

> At last, at even, to my hearth I hark,
>   Still faithful to my sorrow. And inside
>   Even I and all my old magnanimous pride
> Are broken down before her in the dark.
>
> Sorrow's bare arm about my neck doth strain,
>   Sorrow doth lift me to her living mouth
>   And whispers, fierce and loving like the South,
> Saying, 'Dear Pilgrim, have you come again?
>
> 'Whether you walked by wastes of upland green,
>   Whether you walked by wastes of ocean blue,
>   Have you not felt me step by step with you,
> A thing that was both certain and unseen?
>
> 'Or haply is it ended? haply you,
>   Conquering and wholly cured of loving me,
>   Are but a wavering lover who would be
> Off with the old love ere he take the new?'
>
> But, seeing my head did but in silence sink
>   Before her ruthless irony and strong,
> She gave me then that dreadful kiss to drink
>   That is the bitter spring of art and song.
>
> Then with strange gentleness she said, 'I choose
>   To be thine only, thine in all ways; yes,
> Thy daughter and thy sister and thy muse,
>   Thy wife and thine immortal ancestress.

'Feed not thy hate against my rule and rod,
    For I am very clean, my son, and sane,
Because I bring all brave hearts back to God,
    In my embraces being born again.'

Thus spake she low and rocked me like a child,
    And as I stared at her, as stunned awhile,
On her stern face there fell more slow and mild
    The splendour of a supernatural smile.

# CHESTERTON ON 'MAGIC'

[*Magic* (30) was published on the day of the opening performance at the Little Theatre, London, 7 November 1913. The following criticism of his own play was contributed by Chesterton to a symposium, 'Notes on Recent Books by Their Writers' in the *Dublin Review* (520), January 1914.]

The author of *Magic* ought to be told plainly that his play, like most other efforts of that person, has been treated with far too much indulgence in the public press. I will glide mercifully over the most glaring errors, which the critics have overlooked —as that no Irishman could become so complete a cad merely by going to America—that no young lady would walk about in the rain so soon before it was necessary to dress for dinner— that no young man, however American, could run round a Duke's grounds in the time between one bad epigram and another—that Dukes never allow the middle classes to encroach on their gardens so as to permit a doctor's lamp to be seen there—that no sister, however eccentric, could conduct a slightly frivolous love-scene with a brother going mad in the next room—that the Secretary disappears half way through the play without explaining himself; and the conjurer disappears at the end, with almost equal dignity. Such are the candid criticisms I should address to Mr G. K. Chesterton, were he my friend. But as I have always found him my worst enemy, I will confine myself to the criticism which seems to me most fundamental and final.

Of course I shall not differ from any of the dramatic critics; I am bursting with pride to think that I am (for the first time) a dramatic critic myself. Besides, I never argue except when I am right. It is rather a curious coincidence that in every controversy in which I have been hitherto, I have always been entirely right. But if I pretended for one moment that *Magic* was not a pretty badly written play, I should be entirely wrong. I may be allowed to point out the secret of its badness.

By the exercise of that knowledge of all human hearts which descends on any man (however unworthy) the moment he is a

dramatic critic, I perceive that the author of *Magic* originally
wrote it as a short story. It is a bad play, because it was a good
short story. In a short story of mystery, as in a Sherlock Holmes
story, the author and the hero (or villain) keep the reader out of
the secret. Conan Doyle and Sherlock Holmes knew all about
it; and everybody else feels as silly as Watson. But the drama is
built on that grander secrecy which was called the Greek irony.
In the drama, the audience must know the truth when the
actors do not know it. That is where the drama is truly demo-
cratic: not because the audience shouts, but because it knows—
and is silent. Now I do quite seriously think it is a weakness in
a play like *Magic* that the audience is not in the central secret
from the start. Mr G. S. Street put the point with his usual
unerring simplicity by saying that he could not help feeling dis-
appointed with the conjurer because he had hoped he would
turn into the Devil. If anyone knows any real answer to this
genuine and germane criticism, I will see that it is conveyed to
the author.

There are two more criticisms of which I will take note, because they can best be dealt with by an impartial critic like
myself. The first concerns that paralysis of the mind which
scientists now call Pragmatism, and which is represented in this
play as freezing for an instant the intellect of an Anglican priest.
I know it is ignominious to talk of artistic aims that aim and
do not hit. But the idea of the scepticism of the priest was
perfectly simple. It was that there should be no faith or fancy
left to support the supernatural, but only the experience of it.
There is one man who believes—and he believes so strongly that
he wishes he didn't. In the same way, all the people in *Magic*
are purposely made good: so that there shall be no villain, except the great invisible Villain.

The other criticism which the present critic may criticise is the
frequent observation that a soliloquy is old-fashioned—and by
'old-fashioned' they always mean artificial or unnatural. Now
I should say that a soliloquy is the most natural thing in the
world. It is no more artificial than a conscience; or a habit of
walking about a room. I constantly talk to myself. If a man
does not talk to himself, it is because he is not worth talking to.
Soliloquy is simply the strength and liberty of the soul, without
which each one of us would be like that nobleman in one of the

most brilliant and bizarre of Mr Henry James's tales, who did not exist at all except when others were present. Every man ought to be able to argue with himself. And I have tried to do it in this article.

# THREE LETTERS TO E. V. LUCAS

[Edward Verrall Lucas (1868–1938), author, editor and publisher, made two selections from Chesterton's work: *A Shilling for My Thoughts* (854) and *A Gleaming Cohort* (856) and provided the titles for several of the collections of his essays that were issued by Methuen. Chesterton refers to this in the dedicatory letter, 'To E. V. Lucas' in *G. K. C. as M.C.* (80) to which the following letters, now printed for the first time, provide a footnote.]

# THREE LETTERS TO E. V. LUCAS

Telephone
24 Beaconsfield

Overroads
Aylesbury End
Beaconsfield
Jan. 10th [1917]

My dear Lucas,

Your letter came as a very well-merited reproach; and it is hardly a palliation, though it is really a fact, that it found me almost with the pen in my hand to write to you—or at anyrate, so to speak, the pen behind my ear. Only, as you see, I have been driven by huge accumulations of work (do you know I am now an editor?) to the use of a typewriter; and a typewriter behind one's ear is rather a strained figure of speech. I am quite genuinely enthusiastic about your wonderfully varied and yet unified selection of my stuff; I really had no idea that such stuff could be made so attractive. The title alone is an inspiration like a pun and a poem. Somehow I always feel a fool, and quite indefensible, when I consider myself in a literary light; or think seriously of what the reader would think of my things— except indeed when I am arguing with people. Then it is always they who are indefensible. But I really do think your little book (for I will not call it mine) looks as if it might have been written by quite a clever fellow. I believe the biographers or bibliographers of the future, if they find any trace of me at all, will say something like this; 'Chesterton, Gilbert Keith. From the fragments left by this now forgotten writer it is difficult to understand the cause even of such publicity as he obtained in his own day: nevertheless there is reason to believe that he was not without certain fugitive mental gifts. As Budger truly says "The man who invented the two exquisitely apt titles of *All Things Considered* and *A Shilling for My Thoughts* can have had no contemptible intelligence".' And the grave (I hope) will for ever conceal the secret that they were both invented by you.

Gratefully yours
G. K. Chesterton

101 Holland Rd
W.
Nov. 2nd [1920]

Dear Lucas,

I have been meaning to write to you for a terribly long time, in the rush of things which were only in the brutal business sense more urgent, for nothing could possibly be more important than thanking you for your kind offices to me. It was a case of the printer's devil in the hall; and as I am a sort of editor (of the New Witness) I am sometimes in the condition in which all printers are devils. But I wanted to write to you for two distinct reasons, the first of which ought to have urged me to instant speed, and the second of which is my only vague excuse for delay. For the first, I confess it seems to me almost intolerable that you, who write such beautiful essays yourself, should have wasted your time over putting into shape such shapeless essays as mine, which were never originally anything but a sort of printed pattern round a portrait of a bishop or an admiral in the *Illustrated London News*. But there is so much magic about your tact in these things that with your selection and your title they really look as if they were essays; or essays at essays, so to speak. Honestly I wish you had had something less clumsy to control. I feel like Admetus when Apollo herded his hulking cattle.

But my other reason for wanting to write, which is also my half excuse for being so slow in writing, came into my mind quite independently of my own unhappy articles. The truth is, I had a sort of hope of writing you a letter that should be a really good essay, by way of a change. It was to have been a literary appreciation, an appreciation of your last book; and now I have the chance I find my words are quite inadequate to appreciate it. I always admired those books of yours, in that very original scrapbook style of 'Over Bemerton's'. But I do really think 'Verena In The Midst' is the best thing you ever did, and therefore the best of that sort that anybody could do; for nobody else can do that sort of thing but yourself. It seems to me something better than a good novel; it is human characters caught in attitudes more natural than is possible in the plot of any novel, and yet treated so lightly as to have the effect of something fanciful and even farcical. It is beyond me how anybody can get the effect of fantasy within the four corners of probability. And then people in an ordinary story have to talk about the story; whereas your people can talk about things, the things that interest them, as real people do. I am especially devoted to the boy who made the discovery about the two deadly poisons, and for whom that chemical fact filled the whole universe. This is a very inadequate essay, or even short notice, as the journalists say; but it is a very sincere expression of thanks.

Yours sincerely<br>G. K. Chesterton

Telephone                                                    Top Meadow
Beaconsfield 104                                             Beaconsfield
                                                             4th October, 26

Dear Lucas,

I need not inform you that I deserve to be burned alive (a fact of which you are vividly aware) for not having written this letter long before. There is a cause in this case (I cannot call it a reason) which will convey vividly my abject state and abject apology. You know what a foul correspondent I am; and perhaps you do not know what a foul thing my correspondence would be, even for a good correspondent. But for the last two or three weeks it has gone beyond unwillingly neglecting things. It has come to not knowing they were there to neglect. Between a prolonged crisis of my funny little paper and despairing toils to make The Outline of Sanity obtain some sort of outline and some appearance of being sane (I have had to re-write and add enormously for your credit and mine) I was actually sunk so many fathoms deep in a sea of ink that I could not even see the things happening in the world. I never read a newspaper; I never opened the packages sent to me and they piled up into a tower. Somebody asked me what I thought of Cobham and I had never heard of him. And what is worse, I never even knew that the Cohort existed on this earth until about the time I got your letter. I need not say that I do not shine in the matter of the Gleaming Cohort and that I was, as I say, more than a week late in attempting to follow the Gleam. How you can in any case have the patience to reduce my ragged soldiers to such splendid discipline, so that they show so well on parade, I never can imagine. You always make me feel as if my stuff must be much better than it really is; until I start reading it, of course; and even then I always know you have chosen the best. Your very titles are better than my essays; and I always have a dreadful feeling that posterity will write 'The only witty utterances of a high order attributed to this over-rated author are the two titles of "All Things Considered" and "A Shilling for my Thoughts".' And you will lie in the grave and groan and I shall lie in the grave and quake, awaiting the Day of Judgment. I am afraid that all my thanks are swallowed up in apologies; for I have hardly the right to praise a good deed till I have been pardoned for a bad one. But I do most warmly and sincerely thank you, not for the first time.

Yours very sincerely

G. K. Chesterton

# DICKENS AND CHRISTMAS

[The text, hitherto unpublished, of a broadcast to the U.S.A., 25 December 1931. The passages in square brackets were omitted from the broadcast to keep within the time limit of 15 minutes.]

I have been asked to speak to you for a quarter of an hour on Dickens and Christmas; or, as I should prefer to say, on Christmas and Dickens. Why have I been asked to speak to you on Christmas and Dickens? Perhaps the official organisers do not know me very well. Perhaps they have a grudge against you. Why, on this day of holiday, am I made to work? Why, on this day of rejoicing, are you made to suffer? Like everything connected with the mystery of suffering, it is profoundly mysterious. Perhaps, as my remarks proceed, the mystery will grow darker and deeper; and, at the end you will ask yet more wildly, 'Why, O why was he asked to speak about Christmas and Dickens?' On the other hand, I, for my part, cannot help cherishing a faint hope that by the end of my remarks you may have some dim idea of what I am talking about, and why I am talking it. Anyhow, I am going to set myself to answer the question; or rather the two questions, Why Christmas and why Dickens? They are both things that many people think very old-fashioned. But nobody, just yet, thinks the Wireless old-fashioned. Why is it that the officials of the Wireless want to have somebody, anybody, even me, talking about Dickens on Christmas Day?

I will make two answers as simple as the two questions. We talk about Christmas because there is nothing else to talk about. We talk about Dickens because there is nobody else to talk about. I mean that there is no occasion, no date, no day, that has been able to do what Christmas does; and there is no writer, among all our brilliant modern writers, who has been able to do what Dickens did. There are any number of interesting institutions and social functions and so on, but nothing that can be a substitute for Christmas. There are any number of humorists, of witty writers and the rest, but nobody who can be a substitute for Dickens. That is the double proposition I propose to prove to you in fifteen minutes—or now rather less.

First, there is no other festival to keep except Christmas. No new religion has made a new festival. No new philosophy has been sufficiently popular to make a popular holiday. We all know that there are any number of pleasure-seekers in the world today, who think of nothing but amusement; but they do not count. They never have holidays, because they have nothing but holidays. But even they have never made a fixed occasion or form of festivity. It is often said that these pleasure-seekers are Pagans, and that all their life of jazz and cocktails is a life of Paganism. This seems to me a harsh judgment. I mean it seems to me very harsh to Paganism. The Pagan gods and poets of the past were never so cheap or tenth-rate as the fast sets and smart people of the present. Venus was never so vulgar as what they now call Sex Appeal. Cupid was never so coarse and common as a modern realistic novel. The old Pagans were imaginative and creative; they made things and built things. Somehow that habit went out of the world; the power of making feasts and shrines to Nature. Americans we know, are a nation of un-adulterated water-drinkers; but it has never occurred to them to worship Niagara. If any ancient Greek had been a water-drinker, he would have worshipped Niagara on the spot. If we were Pagans, we should be content with nothing less than worship of Beauty. We shouldn't be content with photographs of Film Stars. If we were Pagans there would be a Temple of Venus at Hollywood. If we were Pagans, there would be a Temple of Bacchus; probably in Milwaukee. Even the financiers had a god in those days. There would be a Temple of Mercury, who was the god of commerce, at the end of Wall Street. I admit that, by a curious coincidence, he was also the god of theft. Perhaps that is why he is generally presented to us as the Flying Mercury. But anyhow, the point is that Paganism *could* make things; it could make festivals and festive days; it could make an alternative to Christmas, if it were still alive. But the modern Pagans cannot. The modern Pagans are merely atheists; who worship nothing and therefore create nothing. They could not, for instance, even make a substitute for Thanksgiving Day. For half of them are pessimists who say they have nothing to be thankful for; and the other half are atheists who have nobody to thank. Now you know all about those intellectual rebels who are called Radicals in your country and Revolutionists in mine. You know that they have their virtues as well as their vices, and

that for certain destructive purposes they are often valuable.
But they have no constructive purposes, and certainly no pur-
pose of constructing anything like Christmas. Thus, for instance, I admire Mr Mencken in many ways and Mr Mencken
admires Nietzsche in all sorts of ways; sometimes in quite
extraordinary ways. But, if I may say so, Mr Mencken does not
admire Nietzsche in a festive way. He does not admire him in
a Christmas way. Mr Mencken does not go about singing carols
in the snow, outside other people's houses, to celebrate the day
when Nietzsche was born; or the day he went mad, or whatever
is supposed to be the sacred date. Nietzsche said he was Anti-
Christ. But Mr Mencken has not yet started giving presents to
his family on a festival called Antichristmas. Or again, much has
been said of late of Mr Dreiser; and many admire his very able
work. But however jovial and rollicking Mr Dreiser's philosophy may be, we do not exactly expect him to come down the
chimney, like Santa Claus. The modern Pagans have failed to
do exactly what the ancient Pagans did. They have failed to
make a Feast. Therefore, I repeat, there is nothing to talk about
except Christmas.

In the same way, there is nobody to talk about except Dickens.
There are any number of other people to praise, for various
powers of invention or imagination or satire. There are the
Realists, for instance; and I hope nobody is so unfair to the
Realists as to suppose that they describe real life; especially their
own real life. Realists exaggerate, just as Dickens exaggerated.
But Dickens is still absolutely the only man who exaggerates
high spirits. Dickens is still the only man who exaggerates
happiness. That is, he is the only person to be talked about at
Christmas; because he was the only person who talked about
Christmas as if it was Christmas; as if it was even more Christmas than it is. Now if you think of all the clever modern
writers you admire, you will not admire them less, but you will
see exactly what I mean. They do not exaggerate enjoyment.
If they exaggerate anything, it is despair; it is the spirit of death.
You have read, as I have read, countless current descriptions of
gay young people dancing in night clubs and drinking cocktails. But you were not sure it made you happy. You were not
even sure it made them happy. In Dickens you will find horrible
hypocrites, degrading tricks and conspiracies; but they will

make you happy. Let me take a parallel. Mr Sinclair Lewis in *Elmer Gantry* has described a scandalous Gospel minister. Dickens in *Pickwick* also described a scandalous Gospel minister; Mr Stiggins, known as The Red-Nosed Man. When Sam Weller is in prison, Mr Stiggins and Mrs Weller, his devout admirer, come to visit and console him. They sit on each side of the fire drinking rum, and uttering hollow groans at intervals. Old Mr Weller, the father, suddenly remarks: 'Vell, Samivel, I hope you feel your spirits rose by this 'ere friendly visit'. Now the extraordinary thing is that we *do* feel our spirits rose. Something in the utter idiocy of this form of consolation does really make us happy. The red-nosed man is a deplorable object; but we do not merely deplore. The rum he drinks does not seem to cheer him up; but it cheers us up. His red nose is ridiculous but not repulsive. Now turn from that to any modern novel in which, very probably, the heroine will be a restless spirit whose artistic temperament rebels against the ugliness of her surroundings. She will rebel against the ugliness of her Uncle William's red nose, which will be described in repulsive detail. You know the style of modern writing. 'What had life to offer her? Would that red nose be always there? Would that red nose thrust itself for ever between her and all delicate, all exquisite things?' Anyhow, the heroine is not happy. But, what is more important, the reader is not happy. The reader may see many aspects or take various sides. He may sympathise with the heroine, who, after all, cannot help having an artistic temperament. It is barely possible that he may sympathise with Uncle William; who, after all, cannot help having a red nose. The only point I emphasise is that in either case our sympathy will take the form of sorrow. Anyhow, it will not take the form of joy. No modern novel ever gives us joy out of the uncle's nose or the niece's temperament. Nobody has discovered Dickens's secret of getting joy out of these things and I repeat that no other novelist exists at this season of enjoyment.

I will take another example. I will take a subject on which I trust I am not unduly sensitive; the subject of fat men. I have recently read in a modern novel [a typical passage of the sort I referred to in relation to the red nose. In this case also some sensitive spirit could not endure existence because her surroundings were ugly. People often are; even sensitive spirits sometimes are; but they are so sensitive that nobody tells them so. In this novel there was] a description of some indefensible old gentleman, some intolerable grandfather or unbearable great-uncle, gradually settling down into an armchair. [Need I say that he slouched into it with the sluggish movement of mud? Need I say that he quaked like a quagmire?] Need I say that he presented to the artistic temperament the image of some shapeless monster of the slime? This is quite correct; it may even be quite artistic; but it is not gay. It does not especially cheer us up, even at Christmas. In a word, it is not *funny*. Now let me turn to Dickens; and make a perfectly fair comparison. Sam Weller tells a story entirely devoted to the subject of a Fat Man. After explaining that the gentleman had not seen his own legs for years, he adds with impressive solemnity: 'If you 'ad put an exact model of 'is legs on the table in front of 'im, 'e wouldn't 'ave known 'em by sight'.

Now that is a poem. It uplifts the heart. It might naturally add to the joy of Christmas Day; or any day. It is actually much more of an exaggeration than the pessimist exaggeration [which compares the old man to mud or a monster of the slime]. But it is not only exaggerative; it is also creative. It is a new angle; we might say a new artistic vision. There is something aboriginally absurd in the idea of the old gentleman staring wild-eyed at his own legs; and half recalling something familiar about them; as if he were revisiting the landscape of his youth. [There is something startlingly funny about the idea of a man's own legs being like a sort of public monument that he could never hope to see; and could only admire in an artistic reproduction.] Now that is the essential quality that made Dickens great. He exaggerated, in the sense of making things [greater than they were; but in the sense of making them more ridiculous than they were;] more laughable than they were; more enjoyable than they were. [He took common things and turned them into comic things; but the point is that the comedy was really a Christmas pantomime. It was an occasion for enjoyment and it was enjoyed.] It makes the reader happier; just as if one of the lost and visionary legs had actually been thrust into his own Christmas stocking. Now I defy anybody to say that even the best of the modern satirical writers makes the reader happier. I deny that *Elmer Gantry* is a Christmas present. I deny that anybody wants Mr Dreiser thrust into his Christmas stocking. These works and these authors have all sorts of other valuable qualities, no doubt, but I am talking about Christmas; and why it is that people want to talk about Dickens at Christmas. The reason is in two sentences. The thing he did may or may not be suitable for all purposes; but it is suitable for Christmas. The thing he did may or may not be superior in all respects; but it has never been done since.

I apologise. That is why this dreadful accident has occurred. That is why there has been this disgusting interruption of your Christmas Day; and, I will add, this equally disgusting interruption of my Christmas Day. It is because the most modern of modern people, wielding the most modern and amazing of all forms of scientific machinery—the magic machine which can even do without a machine—is here set to work to carry for so many thousands of miles these two familiar or antiquated names: the name of a feast founded nearly a thousand years ago; the name of a man born more than a hundred years ago. The answer is the answer I have given. It is not because they are superior to their rivals. It is because they have no rivals. The particular achievement they represent has not since been achieved, or even attempted. The particular thing they did men are not even trying to do. If a man wants other things, no doubt he will look for other things; and in these days have no difficulty in finding them. If a man wants to worship the Life Force merely because it is a Force, he may very naturally worship it in the electric battery. I am tempted to say it will serve him right if he eventually worships the life force in the electric chair. But if he wants to worship life because it is living, he will find nothing in history so living as that little life that began in the cave at Bethlehem and now visibly lives for ever. And if he is looking, in a lighter sense, for what is living in all literature— then he may find many descriptions of life more exact or subtle or analytical than that of Dickens; but he will find nothing in all literature so utterly alive. Dickens was separated by centuries of misunderstanding from that mysterious revelation that brought joy upon the earth; but at least he was resolved to enjoy it. It is because Dickens did hand on that tradition of joy, even if it was only traditional, that his name can never be separated from that greater name to which he also was loyal, in an uncongenial time, by an instinct that was almost inspiration. He knew enough about it to enjoy it; and to enjoy himself; and now, in the name of all such things, let us all go and do the same.

# BALLADE OF A MORBID MODERN

(after reading many reminiscences)

[From *G. K.'s Weekly*, 9 November 1933]

I shun my kind. In shame I hang my head
When Giggles takes me to the Plotless Play;
I dread my dreadful secret may be read
At the *Green Toad*, the *Gripes*, the old *Death-Ray*,
The *Nightmare Night-Club*; blind I stare and say
As old Rankeillor to his servant Torrance
(What, you read *Stevenson* . . . hush! Whispers pray)
*I'm getting rather tired of D. H. Lawrence.*

Oh what he said she said they said he said!
Oh what she says he said she said they say!
. . . We are grown men; and born and bred and wed
Not quite in sunder from the common clay;
We read plain words with which the street-boys play
Without much admiration or abhorrence
But what the devil does it *matter* . . . eh?
I'm getting rather tired of D. H. Lawrence.

Not mightier are the minds in being misled
Who miss the front-door or mistake the day
And break through gutters and back-drains instead;
Perhaps the only way—but not the way.
Nor mock I dirt or doubt or disarray,
But when their gutters flood the house in torrents
(a modern rhyme) I mention, if I may,
I'm getting rather tired of D. H. Lawrence.

### *Envoi*

Prince, *fortes ante Agamemnona,*
A man named Alighieri lived in Florence
And William Shakspur lived down Warwick way—
I'm getting rather tired of D. H. Lawrence.

# THE GOOD GROCER

## (An Apology)

[This poem was published in *Princess Elizabeth's Gift Book* (402) in 1935]

Babes, when I too was young and always right
And tangled in that not unrighteous fight
Beneath the Wooden Flag, the Painted Sign,
We poured our blood—or anyhow our wine—
For feast of all our fathers, and liberties;
Not having Charity before my eyes
I cursed a Grocer . . . saying that he, by fault,
Put sand in sugar and no salt in salt,
Trapped men with stinking fish that leapt from tins;
And rising to the toppling top of sins
Discouraged Pubs and spoilt the English Inns.


The Heavens, I learn as still I linger and live,
Punish more generously than men forgive,
No grinning Grocer slew me with a sweet,
I writhed across no tins of poisoned meat;
Only . . . where far in the warm western shires
Steep stooping woods are dipped in sunset fires
The children told me that, aloof, alone,
Dwelt the Good Grocer whom I had not known.


Ah, not forgotten, the children that I knew,
Not if they died—not even if they grew—
How their locks flamed and limbs like arrows sped
And faces shone with the wild news they said:
The Fairy Grocer—his were magic sales,
His books might have been filled with fairy tales;
He might have tipped sardines back in the sea,
Given all his goods away with a pound of tea;
Sanding no sugar, on the other hand,
Have spread his sugar o'er the shores for sand:

Till children came unto those yellow sands
And there took hands—and handfuls in their hands
And mouthfuls in their mouths; stuffed more and more
Till they had made erosion of the shore,
Bit bays and inlets out of all the coast
Like giant bites out of titanic toast.

To you dear children of old days, I send
This apologia to your early friend,
You know, though I said salt was dust in mirth,
Our dust can still be salt, and salt of the earth;
A Wizard is an easier thing to be
Than being a Good Grocer, as is he.

# COMFORT FOR COMMUNISTS

[*G. K.'s Weekly*, 11 July 1935]

In January of last year Bezboznik complained that anti-religious Soviets had been disbanded in seventy districts, while it had been thought that in the region of Kovrov there was a whole system of atheist cells, the President of that region wrote . . . that neither in the town nor in the region were there any cells left—in fact 'in the entire district there is now only one organised atheist—myself.'
From an article by Father C. C. Martindale S.J., in the *Catholic Herald*, 11 May 1935.


'I'm all alone; I can't organise anyone,
There's nobody left to organise me,
And still I'm the only organised atheist
In all the province of Skuntz (E.C.).


Sometimes disgusting organised atheists
Orphan the stars without permit from me,
Unmake their Maker without their ticket
Or their copy of Form X.793.


The Blasphemy Drill's getting slacker and slacker,
Free Thought is becoming alarmingly free,
And I'll be the only organised atheist
Between the Bug and the big Black Sea.'

&#9733; &#9733; &#9733;

Ours, ours is the key O desolate crier,
The golden key to what ills distress you
Left without ever a God to judge you,
Lost without even a Man to oppress you.


Look west, look west to the Land of Profits,
To the old gold marts, and confess it then
How greatly your great propaganda prospers
When left to the methods of Business Men.

Ah, Mammon is mightier than Marx in making
A goose-step order for godless geese,
And snobs know better than mobs to measure
Where Golf shall flourish and God shall cease.

Lift up your hearts in the wastes Slavonian,
Let no Red Sun on your wrath go down;
There are millions of very much organised atheists
In the Outer Circle of London town.

# TRUE SYMPATHY

## or

# PREVENTION OF CRUELTY TO TEACHERS

[From the *Catholic Herald*, 15 December 1939, where it appeared with
the following Editorial Note: 'G. K. Chesterton wrote this poem for
a very young friend of his and now, after many years, the little friend,
quite beyond the algebra stage, allows us to publish these verses for the
first time.']

> I was kind to all my masters
>   And I never worked them hard
> To goad them to exactitude
>   Or speaking by the card.

> If one of them should have the air
>   Of talking through his hat
> And call a curve isosceles
>   I let it go at that.

> The point was without magnitude;
>   I knew without regret
> Our minds were moving parallel
>   Because they never met.

> Because I could not bear to make
>   An Algebraist cry
> I gazed with interest at X
>   And never thought of Why.

> That he should think I thought he thought
>   That X was A B C
> Was far, far happier for him
>   And possibly for me.

While other teachers raved and died
   In reason's wild career,
Men who had driven themselves mad
   By making themselves clear,

My teachers laugh and sing and dance,
   Aged, but still alive;
Because I often let them say
   That two and two are five.

Angles obtuse appeared acute,
   Angles acute were quite
Obtuse; but I was more obtuse:
   Their angles were all right.

I wore my Soul's Awakening smile
   I felt it was my duty:
Lo! Logic works by Barbara
   And life is ruled by Beauty.

And Mathematics merged and met
   Its Higher Unity,
Where Five and Two and Twelve and Four
   They all were One to me.

# TO THE JESUITS

## (Spain, 1936)

[This, Chesterton's last poem, was written for the Jesuits and the manuscript given to Father Corbishley S.J., of Campion Hall, Oxford.
It was published in G. K.'s Weekly, 26 March 1936 and in the Catholic
Herald, 27 September 1940. It is here collected for the first time and
printed by kind permission of the Master of Campion Hall.]

Flower-wreathed with all unfading calumnies
Scarlet and splendid with eternal slander
How should you hope, where'er the world may wander,
To lose the long laudation of its lies?

The yellow gods of sunrise saw arise
Your tilted towers that housed the moons and suns,
The red sons of the sunset, not with guns
But with guitars, you ambushed for surprise.

You bade the Red Man rise like the Red Clay
Of God's great Adam in his human right,
Till trailed the snake of trade, our own time's blight,
And Man lost Paradise in Paraguay.

You, when wild sects tortured and mocked each other
Saw truth in the wild tribes that tortured you
Slurred for not slurring all who slurred or slew,
Blamed that your murderer was too much your brother

You hailed before its dawn Democracy
Which in its death bays you with demagogues
You dared strong kings that hunted you with dogs
To hide some hunted king in trench or tree.

When Calvin's Christ made Antichrist had caught
Even the elect and all men's hearts were hardened,
You were called profligates because you pardoned
And tools of ignorance because you taught.

All that warped world your charity could heal
All the world's charity was not for you;
How should you hope deliverance in things new
In this the last chance twist of the world's wheel?

One, while that wheel as a vast top is twirled
With every age, realm, riot, pomp or pact,
Thrown down in thunder like a cataract,
Said, 'Fear not; I have overthrown the world'.

# INDEX

*Note:* Numerical references are to pages, not sections.

The titles of works by Chesterton himself are printed in small capitals, e.g. AVOWALS AND DENIALS.